Harold Pinter

THE BIRTHDAY PARTY

Educational Text

Edited and with
an Introduction by
Margaret Rose

faber and faber
LONDON · BOSTON

The Birthday Party first published in 1960 by Eyre Methuen
Paperback edition first published in 1991 by
Faber and Faber Limited
This educational edition first published in 1993 by
Faber and Faber Limited
3 Queen Square London WC1N 3AU

Photoset by Parker Typesetting Service, Leicester
Printed by Clays Ltd, St Ives plc

A CIP record of this book is available from the British Library

ISBN 0–571–16734–9

2 4 6 8 10 9 7 5 3 1

Contents

Introduction

Harold Pinter's Life and Works

Harold Pinter was born in Hackney, east London, on 10 October 1930, the only son of Jewish parents, Frances (Mann) and Hyman (Jack) Pinter. His father was a hard-working tailor.

The 1930s saw the growth of the Fascist Party in Great Britain, and in certain areas of London, particularly the East End, there were frequent clashes between militant Jews and Communists, on the one hand, and Fascists, on the other. In 1932, Oswald Mosley founded the British Union of Fascists, which was very active in the East End.

With the outbreak of the Second World War, Pinter was evacuated to Cornwall in 1939 and stayed there a year. In 1942 he was evacuated again from London, this time to Reading, where he stayed nine months. He attended Hackney Downs Grammar School, where he excelled in English literature, drama and sports. According to later recollections, it was after the Second World War, with the rise of the young Fascists in England from 1946 to 1948, that awareness of the Gestapo and Nazism began; in his youth he was frequently caught up in fights.

In 1948 Pinter obtained a grant to attend the Royal Academy of Dramatic Art (RADA), one of the most prestigious drama schools in Britain. However, he felt painfully out of place and left before the end of his first year.

In 1948 he was called up for National Service. Although not a pacifist, he objected strongly to the Cold War and could see no point in military action at that particular time. He declared himself a conscientious objector, and as a result faced two trials, was found guilty and fined £80 instead of being sent to prison. He returned to drama school, this time to the Central School of Speech and Drama.

Under the name of Harold Pinta, two of his poems appeared in 1950 in *Poetry London*. The same year he joined the company of actor-manager Anew McMaster, who left a lasting impression upon him (see 'Mac' in *Plays: Three*). From 1951 to 1952 Pinter toured Ireland, playing a number of different roles in classical theatre (Sophocles and Shakespeare), comedies and mysteries (Oscar Wilde and Agatha Christie).

In 1953 he joined Donald Wolfit's repertory company, and met his future wife, actress Vivien Merchant. Both played in Shakespeare's *As You Like It*. For the next three years, he continued to tour, adopting the stage name of David Baron. He also did a variety of odd-jobs; he was a ticket collector at the Astoria dance hall, a waiter, a doorman, a dishwasher, a snow-shoveller and a door-to-door salesman. In 1956 he and Merchant married.

1957
Pinter's first play, *The Room*, was staged by the University of Bristol Drama Department.

1958
In April *The Birthday Party* was produced at the Arts Theatre in Cambridge, and in May it moved to the Lyric Theatre, Hammersmith, west London. Most critics hated the play, and it closed down after a week. Only Harold Hobson, drama critic of the *Sunday Times*, expressed

enthusiasm: 'Mr Pinter, on the evidence of this work, possesses the most original, disturbing and arresting talent in theatrical London.'

That winter Pinter composed *The Hothouse*, but he did not allow it to be staged or published until 1980.

1959

The Dumb Waiter was premièred in Germany. Pinter's radio play, *A Slight Ache*, was broadcast by the BBC.

1960

Pinter directed the London productions of *The Room* and *The Dumb Waiter*, starring Vivien Merchant and Henry Woolf, at the Hampstead Theatre Club. *The Caretaker* was Pinter's first commercial success. After opening at the Arts Theatre, London, it transferred to the Duchess Theatre, London (starring Alan Bates, Peter Woodthorpe and Donald Pleasence). The play won an Evening Standard Award. *A Night Out* was broadcast on both television and radio and *Night School* on television.

1961

A Slight Ache was staged at the Arts Theatre. Pinter played the part of Mick in the final month of *The Caretaker* in London. It closed after 425 performances. *The Caretaker* opened in New York and received good reviews.

1962

Pinter began a long collaboration with director Peter Hall. They directed *The Collection* for the Royal Shakespeare Company. Pinter wrote the screenplay of *The Caretaker* and adapted Robin Maugham's novel *The Servant* for a film directed by Joseph Losey. In 1962 he also wrote *The Lover* for television.

1963

The Lover was staged at the Arts Theatre, in a double bill with *The Dwarfs* (Pinter co-directed). *The Lover* was televised and won the Italia Prize and British TV Producers and Directors Award. He wrote a screenplay based on Penelope Mortimer's novel *The Pumpkin Eater*.

1964

Pinter wrote *The Homecoming* and directed the Royal Shakespeare Company's production of *The Birthday Party*. He won the New York Film Critics Award for *The Servant*, which was entered in the Venice Film Festival.

1965

The Homecoming was staged by the Royal Shakespeare Company. *The Tea Party* was televised. Pinter received the British Academy Award for *The Pumpkin Eater*.

1966

The film of Pinter's screenplay *The Quiller Memorandum* was directed by Michael Anderson. *Night School* was broadcast on the radio.

1967

The Birthday Party and *The Homecoming* opened in New York to great acclaim. The latter won the Tony Award for the best play on Broadway. Pinter wrote the screenplay *Accident*, based on Nicholas Mosley's novel. The film, directed by Losey, received the Cannes Jury Prize. Pinter directed Robert Shaw's *The Man in the Glass Booth* in London and his *The Basement* was televised.

1968

Landscape was temporarily censored because Pinter refused to make textual cuts which were required by the Lord Chamberlain's Office.

1969

Silence and *Landscape* were staged at the Aldwych Theatre, London. Pinter wrote the screenplay based on L. P. Hartley's novel *The Go-Between*. Once again, Losey directed the film.

1970

Pinter composed *Old Times*. He directed James Joyce's *Exiles* at the Mermaid Theatre, London. He was awarded the Hamburg Shakespeare Prize and *The Basement* was staged. He also wrote the screenplay for *Langrishe, Go Down*. He received an Hon. D.Litt. from Reading University – the first of several doctorates.

1971

Old Times was presented in London and New York. Pinter directed Simon Gray's *Butley* in Oxford and London. He also won the Writers' Guild Award and the Cannes Film Festival Golden Palm Award for *The Go-Between*.

1972

He wrote a short piece, *Monologue*, for television and worked with Losey on the screenplay of Marcel Proust's *A la recherche du temps perdu*.

1973

Pinter directed his first film, based on his screenplay of *Butley*. He publicly stated his position concerning US support of the overthrow of Allende in Chile. He was appointed by Peter Hall as an associate director of the National Theatre, London, and *Monologue* was televised.

1974

Pinter wrote *No Man's Land* and the screenplay of *The Last Tycoon*. He directed John Hopkin's *Next of Kin* at the National Theatre.

1975

Pinter directed Simon Gray's *Otherwise Engaged*. *No Man's Land* was staged at the Old Vic, London, with Ralph Richardson and John Gielgud.

1976

Pinter directed Noël Coward's *Blithe Spirit* at the National Theatre and, in New York, William Archibald's *The Innocents* and Simon Gray's *Otherwise Engaged*. He acted in the radio production of Samuel Beckett's *Rough for Radio*.

1977

He acted in *Two Plays* by Vaclav Havel.

1978

Betrayal was produced at the National Theatre. Pinter directed Simon Gray's *The Rear Column* and *No Man's Land* was televised.

1980

Pinter and Vivien Merchant divorced. Pinter married Lady Antonia Fraser.

Pinter directed *The Hothouse* at the Hampstead Theatre. He donated the proceeds from his birthday celebrations at the National Theatre to Vaclav Havel, who was imprisoned. Pinter wrote the screenplay based on John Fowles's novel *The French Lieutenant's Woman*.

1981
Family Voices was broadcast on BBC radio and later staged at the National Theatre. He wrote the screenplay of *Betrayal*.

1982
A Kind of Alaska, *Victoria Station* and *Family Voices* were staged in a triple-bill, called *Other Places*, at the National Theatre. He wrote the screenplay *Victory* from the novel by Joseph Conrad.

1983
Pinter directed Jean Giraudoux's *The Trojan War Will Not Take Place* at the National Theatre.

1984
One for the Road was directed by Pinter at the Lyric Theatre Studio, Hammersmith. He wrote the screenplay of *Turtle Diary*.

1985
Other Places, now consisting of *Victoria Station*, *Family Voices* and *One for the Road*, opened at the Duchess Theatre, London. On behalf of International PEN, Pinter and Arthur Miller travelled to Turkey to show their solidarity with dissident writers. They presented a petition signed by 2,330 writers, scientists and churchmen, demanding respect for human rights. *One for the Road* was televised.

1986

Pinter and Lady Antonia, along with Margaret Drabble, John Mortimer, Salman Rushdie and others, founded the June 20th Society to express their opposition to Thatcherism. Pinter and Liv Ullmann starred in an American tour of *Old Times*.

1987

Pinter began the screenplay from Margaret Atwood's novel *The Handmaid's Tale*. He played Goldberg in the BBC production of *The Birthday Party*.

Pinter founded the Arts for Nicaragua Fund.

1988

Pinter's play *Mountain Language* was televised. Pinter directed the production at the National Theatre. He wrote the screenplay for *The Heat of the Day*, based on Elizabeth Bowen's novel.

Pinter became an increasingly well-known public speaker on such issues as human rights, British censorship and the government's anti-homosexual policies. He wrote screenplays from Fred Uhlmann's novel *Reunion* and Ian McEwan's *The Comfort of Strangers*.

1989

Mountain Language opened in New York. Pinter set to work on Kafka's *The Trial*.

1990

Pinter delivered a speech at the Institute of Contemporary Arts, London, on behalf of Salman Rushdie, author of *The Satanic Verses*, who had been in hiding since 1989, when Ayatollah Khomeini had issued a call for his death.

1991
Peter Hall directed a revival of *The Homecoming* and Pinter
directed *The Caretaker* at the Comedy Theatre, London, as
part of celebrations for his sixtieth birthday. In April, the
Pinter International Festival was held at Ohio State Uni-
versity, to celebrate his birthday. Pinter sent a new play
for the occasion, *Party Time*. *Party Time* was premièred in
London, with Pinter directing. A new sketch, *New World
Order*, was also premièred in London, at the Theatre
Upstairs, Royal Court.

1992
Pinter directed *Party Time* for television and acted in *No
Man's Land* at the Almeida Theatre.

Background to Pinter's Work

The 1950s and early 1960s saw a deep transformation taking place in British society, and the arts (especially the cinema, the visual arts and the theatre) both helped to bring about and reflected this change. A cultural revolution was on the way, thanks to a wide range of influences such as jazz music, rock 'n' roll, television, and American and French cinema.

HISTORICAL AND POLITICAL EVENTS

In 1951 the Conservative Party came to power, after the immediate postwar enthusiasm for socialist policies waned. The economic prosperity of the 1950s, coupled with the new educational and welfare provisions of the previous Labour government, created a fairly peaceful and stable society, no doubt prompting the Prime Minister, Harold Macmillan, to make his over-optimistic statement, 'The class struggle is over and we have won.'

However, developments both at home and abroad shattered the relative confidence engendered by the calm of the postwar years. In 1956 the British government, together with France and Israel, decided to oppose President Nasser's nationalization of the Suez Canal and invaded Egypt. By December, though, they had been forced to retreat, following a United Nations' ruling – a clear sign that Britain's interests could not override those of other countries. And then, in the same year, the Soviet Union sent forces into Hungary, bringing about another terrible blow to world order.

By the mid-1950s racism had become an increasingly serious problem in Britain. Due to the postwar economic boom many people from the Commonwealth had been encouraged to come to work in Britain. In 1958 in Notting Hill (a district of London) and in the city of Nottingham

there were violent street riots between the black and white
communities, marking the beginning of a long period of
racial unrest.

FREE CINEMA

In the late 1950s, Lindsay Anderson, Karel Reisz and Tony
Richardson were among the directors who changed the
image of British cinema in what became kown as the Free
Cinema movement. The movement, in the words of its
promoters, aimed at creating films that were 'poetic, free
and committed'. In 1956, in the first Free Cinema pro-
gramme, Anderson claimed that their films had to take
contemporary Britain as their focus. While places like a
London jazz club or an East End street might have featured
in films in the past, Free Cinema directors wished to portray
them differently, with love or anger, but never coldly,
ascetically or conventionally. Reisz's *We Are the Lambeth
Boys* (1959) and *Saturday Night and Sunday Morning* (1960),
and Richardson's *A Taste of Honey* (1961), number among
the innovative films of the period.

POSTWAR PAINTING

In the visual arts what is losely known as the 'School of
London' came into existence after the Second World War.
Painters like Francis Bacon, Lucian Freud, Frank Auer-
bach, Leon Kossoff, and Michael Andrews were linked by
their commitment to painting the human figure. The
anguish and alienation present in many of their paintings
would seem to offer a visual counterpart to the world of
Pinter's early theatre.

POSTWAR BRITISH THEATRE

Many postwar dramatists were no longer satisfied with the
staple fare in London's West End – musicals, thrillers and

revues. They felt bored with the polished works of Noël Coward and Terence Rattigan, depicting middle-class concerns, and the verse dramas of T. S. Eliot and Christopher Fry.

In the early 1950s, Pinter had regularly performed in plays by Coward, Eliot and Priestley, as well as in Agatha Christie thrillers. So while, like his peers, he rejected the conventional theatre, the style and structure of his work was none the less deeply influenced by his familiarity with it.

'ANGRY YOUNG MEN'

In 1956 John Osborne's seminal play *Look Back in Anger* (directed by Tony Richardson at the Royal Court Theatre, London) took audiences by surprise. The protagonist is a young man, Jimmy Porter, who, like many working-class people, felt disappointed that the Labour Party's promises of social reform had come to so little. Notwithstanding a university education, Jimmy is unable to communicate with his middle-class wife and her father, a retired colonel. The play, on one level, is a realistic dramatization of the everyday life of two young people in the 1950s. On a broader level, it stands as a critique of the social and political changes taking place in postwar Britain, which was being forced to adjust to a new role without its former Empire.

The media labelled Osborne and his fellow writers 'Angry Young Men', as they chose to look critically at the lot of working-class people in contemporary British society.

EUROPEAN INFLUENCES

In the 1950s, too, British theatre became less insular and more aware of trends in Europe. In 1956, the Berliner Ensemble came to London for the first time with plays by Bertolt Brecht, so introducing the idea of a radical political theatre with a new style of performance. Joan Littlewood's

Theatre Workshop is just one example of the influence Brecht exerted on political dramatists and directors in Britain.

In 1955 another significant event took place when the Arts Theatre staged Eugène Ionesco's *The Lesson* and Samuel Beckett's *Waiting for Godot*. In a seminal study, *The Theatre of the Absurd*, critic Martin Esslin grouped these writers, calling them absurdist dramatists. He claimed that they shared a similar world view. In *Waiting for Godot* Beckett points to the essentially absurd nature of the human condition: his protagonists, Vladimir and Estragon spend their time waiting for something or someone who never arrives. Esslin included Pinter among the absurdist group, and the label stuck for many years.

Today, one needs to reassess Pinter's position. The 'absurdist elements' in his early plays are indisputable: he, like Beckett and Ionesco, points to the ultimate meaninglessness of life, in a world where God does not exist, and, like them, he implicitly raises philosophical questions about the very nature of existence. On the other hand, though, as Pinter himself has recently pointed out, he was never 'a disinterested playwright'. His early works make broad political statements about the life of working-class people in the immediate postwar era.

PINTER: A POST-MODERN WRITER

Pinter is a central figure in the post-modern age. His work underlines the ability of theatre to reflect the elusive nature of reality, and at the same time points to the inadequacy of theatrical representation itself. His dramatic language in particular sensitively emphasizes these issues, making even his early plays, which are culturally specific to Britain in the 1950s, powerful and able to communicate to audiences around the world today.

Pinter's work in different media, and especially his many adaptations of novels for the screen, brings him into the mainstream of late twentieth-century post-modernism.

A Summary of *The Birthday Party*

ACT ONE

Petey enters the living room of his seaside boarding-house and begins reading. The voice of his wife, Meg, can be heard through the kitchen-hatch. As she gives him break-fast, she tries to get him to talk. She asks if Stanley, their lodger, is up yet. Petey mentions two men he met the night before. He says they will be coming to rent a room if Meg has one ready. Meg goes upstairs to wake Stanley.

Offstage her 'wild laughter' and 'shouting' from Stanley can be heard. She comes downstairs, 'panting and arranging her hair'. Petey remains silent. Stanley appears for breakfast and Meg attempts to exploit the breakfast ritual to her own ends. She flirts with Stanley and, at other times, treats him like a child, but he responds by complaining about the food and saying the milk is sour.

She introduces the subject of the two men, and Stanley is obviously worried. He fantasizes about his future tour as a pianist, but immediately after admits that his career has been ruined by people whose names he does not mention. He then frightens Meg with a story about somebody who is coming to the house in a van complete with wheelbarrow to take her away.

Lulu arrives with a parcel and places it on the sideboard. McCann and Goldberg enter, and Stanley manages to escape through a back door, without their seeing him. They look around, trying to decide if this is the house where they have 'a job to do'. Meg arrives and tells them about Stanley, saying that it is his birthday that evening. Goldberg plans a party for nine o'clock. They leave.

Alone with Stanley, Meg tries to reassure him that she will continue looking after him, even if she has two other lodgers. She tells him about the party and gives him the parcel Lulu brought. It is a toy drum. The first act concludes with Stanley parading around the room, beating the drum, first slowly, then in a 'savage and possessed' way.

ACT TWO

Stanley meets McCann, who tells him about the party in his honour. Stanley declines the invitation, saying he prefers to spend an evening in on his own. He tells McCann about his past life, in Maidenhead, where he lived very quietly – an account which contradicts the one he gave Meg. He informs McCann that the house was never a boarding-house and it is not his birthday. Stanley grows angry when McCann refuses to believe him. McCann hits him. Stanley tells McCann that he has come to the house by mistake and that he is being made a fool of by the person who brought him.

Goldberg enters and Stanley tells him to leave. Goldberg refuses, insisting they must celebrate his birthday. Stanley's interrogation begins slowly, with the two intruders asking him a series of disconnected questions. Some are absurd, such as, 'Why did the chicken cross the road?' and some more menacing such as, 'Why did you kill your wife?' As the inquisition grows more aggressive, McCann snatches Stanley's glasses, so that he stumbles round the room, unable to see. Stanley begins to break down, screaming for mercy.

Loud drum beats can be heard offstage. An anticlimax follows as Meg appears, dressed for the party. Stanley utters his last coherent words as he asks for his glasses back. From now on Stanley is silent, lacking all vitality. The party begins with Goldberg flirting with Meg and later with Lulu. As he talks about his past life, he mentions places similar to the ones Stanley spoke of before in connection with his own past.

They decide to play a game of blind-man's buff, with first Meg as the blindman, then Stanley. As Stanley moves slowly round the room, tension mounts. McCann puts the drum on the floor and Stanley falls over it. He gets up, finds Meg and begins to strangle her. McCann and Goldberg throw him off.

A blackout follows, and in the dark McCann shines a torch in Goldberg's face. Then it falls from his hands. In the mounting confusion Stanley gets hold of Lulu. McCann finds the torch and shines it on Stanley, who can be seen bent over Lulu as she is spread-eagled on the table. He is giggling. Goldberg and McCann converge on Stanley, who has flattened himself against the wall.

ACT THREE

Meg and Petey are at breakfast, and she is apologizing because there are no cornflakes left. She remarks on the broken drum and says that when she went to wake Stanley, she found McCann and Goldberg in his room. McCann told her they still had to talk to him. She comments on a big car outside the house and asks Petey if there is a wheelbarrow in it.

Goldberg enters and says that Stanley has had a nervous breakdown as the birthday celebrations were too much for him. McCann comes in with two suitcases, adamant that he is not going back upstairs. He wants to leave, but before doing so he would like, as he puts it, to 'finish the bloody thing'. He gets angry with Goldberg, who seems exhausted after the night's inquisition. Goldberg wants to give him advice about how to get on in life, but is unable to conclude, three times repeating the unfinished: 'I believe that the world . . .'

Lulu enters and McCann treats her badly, telling her to confess. McCann brings Stanley down, dressed in a well-cut suit and holding his broken glasses in his hand. The two inquisitors proceed 'to woo him, gently and with relish', but he does not react. They promise to look after him, in a gradual crescendo, until Stanley starts making loud gurgling noises. When Petey enters, McCann tells him they are taking Stanley away. The three go out. Meg and Petey talk about the party. Meg asks if Stanley is down yet. She remarks what a lovely party it was.

Theme

Pinter's plays, like much modern drama, do not have a complicated plot, but rather the emphasis is on theme. They cannot, moreover, be said to be about any one subject, nor can they be summed up in a single meaning. While, in my opinion, the following themes are central to *The Birthday Party*, they are certainly not exhaustive.

POWER GAMES

A pervasive theme running through Pinter's plays, poetry and many of his screenplays, such as *The Servant* and *The Go-Between*, is man's insatiable need to dominate his fellow man. In *The Birthday Party* he dramatizes human relationships as a battle for dominance, with the characters carefully calculating their opponents' strengths and weaknesses, as if they were players in a hard-fought game (note the many cricket terms in *The Birthday Party*).

Through their interrogation, McCann and Goldberg set out to destroy Stanley, and they have planned for this carefully. Meg plays another and more subtle kind of power game, in her role as would-be mother and mistress to Stanley. It is she who decides when he wakes up and what he eats, and through this domestic ritual she aims to dominate him. Stanley, unlike Petey, refuses to be drawn into Meg's net and makes her understand this by complaining bitterly about the food and drink.

A WORLD OF CRUELTY

On one level, the world of unmotivated cruelty and hate which McCann and Goldberg represent is reminiscent of the atmosphere pervading Franz Kafka's novels, *The Trial* and *The Castle*. K. in *The Trial*, like Stanley, is the victim of strangers who invade his private world, accuse him of an unspecified crime, and seek to undo him. It was this 'unidentified' threat present in *The Birthday Party*, and also in *The Room* and *The Dumb Waiter*, that brought early Pinter critics to define them as 'comedies of menace'. As Pinter put the matter in an interview with Kenneth Tynan in 1960: '[people] are scared of what is outside the room. Outside the room is a world bearing upon them, which is frightening . . . We are all in this, all in a room, and outside is a world . . . which is most inexplicable and frightening, curious and alarming.'

Stanley tells Meg about the anonymous and cruel people who, he claims, 'Carved me up' (page 53) at the concert hall. He also refers to other mysterious individuals who are coming to the house with a van and a wheelbarrow to take Meg away. When Goldberg and McCann arrive, it is unclear whether they are the people Stanley has been referring to. From the start McCann's nervousness about whether they have come to 'the right house' (page 58), and a little later Goldberg's mention of an unspecified job they have to do (page 59), suggest the idea of a secret organization. They later proceed to interrogate Stanley ruthlessly, without clear motivation. In the end, McCann and Goldberg oblige Stanley to leave the security of the room for an unknown outside.

IDENTITY

As Martin Esslin has observed: 'Pinter, like Heidegger, takes as his starting point man's confrontation with himself and the nature of his own being, that fundamental anxiety which is nothing less than a living being's basic awareness of the threat of non-being, of annihilation.'

Pinter's concern with identity in *The Birthday Party* draws him close to Samuel Beckett and other absurdist writers, who consider personality and character as unstable and never completely definable. Stanley's personality is mysterious. At the beginning of the play, he says to Meg: 'Mrs Boles, when you address yourself to me, do you ever ask yourself who exactly you are talking to?' (page 51). He gives different versions of his past life, to Meg and to McCann respectively. During the course of the play, Stanley is in a way 'reborn' – one of the possible reasons for the play's title. Following his inquisition, he no longer seems to be the same person we met at the beginning. The articulate individual who harasses Meg in the initial breakfast scene has turned into a silent and unrecognizable shell of a man in acts two and three.

Goldberg makes no secret of the fact that he has lived under at least three different names. He says that he has been called Simey, Nat and Benny, bringing to mind something Pinter once told Joan Bakewell: 'I'm quite interested in the fact that a good deal of the past is really a mist – my past anyway.' If one cannot verify what happened in the past because of a mist, as Pinter puts it, the idea of a stable identity becomes impossible.

BIRTH AND DEATH

In some ways, *The Birthday Party* may be seen as an allegory
of birth and death. Stanley, the sinful mortal, can be seen as
a modern-day Everyman figure, from medieval morality
plays. He is called upon to die by two Angels of Death
(Goldberg and McCann). In this reading of the play,
Goldberg's statement to Meg, 'If we hadn't come today
we'd have come tomorrow' (page 62), takes on new meaning. Before passing from this earth to another life (a rebirth,
hence the need for the birthday party), like Everyman, Stanley must make atonement for his sins. The interrogation
scene, with Goldberg as a representative of the Jewish
religion and McCann, a Roman Catholic Irishman, can be
seen as a play on Everyman's own ordeal as he prepares for
death. In the final scene, when Stanley comes down the
stairs in a dark suit and white collar, sightless because his
glasses are broken, his silent, lifeless image is similar to that
of a corpse being taken away to a funeral. As in the morality
play, Stanley has not chosen to die; rather, death has very
clearly come to seek him out.

Reading or Watching a Pinter Play

Like the late Samuel Beckett, Pinter has refused to 'explain'
his plays or the psychology of his characters. His theatre has
often been described as 'difficult to understand', 'puzzling',
'a problem', and in the field of Pinter criticism there exist
many often contradictory interpretations of the plays' meanings. *The Birthday Party*, for instance, has been seen as an
exploration of obscure menace and existential anguish,
reminiscent of Kafka's *The Trial*. Another interpretation
sees the play as a kind of initiation ritual, in which Stanley
must be expelled from the room in order to go out into the

world. Yet another considers *The Birthday Party* a dramatic realization of the problem of human communication.

It is important to understand that these different critical points of view are not mutually exclusive; nor can any one of them offer a definitive interpretation. As Martin Esslin maintains, the plays amount to poetic metaphors which lie open to an infinite number of interpretations. In line with post-structuralist criticism, Pinter has encouraged critics to keep an open mind concerning the possible meanings of his plays. As he explained in a letter dated 1960 to Peter Wood, who was directing *The Birthday Party*: 'Meaning begins in the words, in the actions, continues in your head and ends nowhere. There is no end to meaning. Meaning which is resolved, parcelled, labelled and ready for export is dead, impertinent – and meaningless.'

So the reader or spectator of a Pinter play should not expect to find a single key to what the plays are about, but keep in mind that they work on many levels. The dramatist's reluctance to explain his plays derives partly from his particular view of reality and human nature, and partly from his attitude to art (and especially to the theatre), language and, ultimately, silence. For reasons of clarity, I will look at these points separately even if they are actually interconnected.

PINTER'S WORLD VIEW

Like many post-modernist writers, Pinter does not believe in a fixed external reality to which art and language systematically refer. As he said in 1962, in his speech 'Between the Lines':

I think there is a shared common ground all right, but it's more like a quicksand. Because 'reality' is quite a strong firm word, we tend to think, or to hope, that the state to which it refers is equally firm, settled and unequivocal. It does not seem to be, and in my opinion, it's no worse nor better for that.

Consequently, even if Pinter's early theatre is at first sight realistic in its dramatization of familiar situations – life in a seedy boarding-house in the *The Birthday Party*, for example – he undermines our certainty about the places and their inhabitants. His characters reflect the image of 'quicksand'; Goldberg, for instance, has possessed at least three different names; Stanley's past is described in different ways, according to his questioner.

PINTER'S CREATIVE PROCESS

Pinter's plays do not spring exclusively from his imagination. Talking about *The Room* and *The Caretaker*, he explained in a letter to Peter Wood how he started from a real-life experience: 'The germs of my plays? I'll be as accurate as I can about that. I went in a room and saw one person standing up and one person sitting down and a few weeks later I wrote *The Room*. I went into another room and saw two people standing up and I wrote *The Caretaker*.' In an interview with Lawrence Bensky in 1966 in which he described his early days in rep, he recalled: 'an obscene household, cats, dogs, filth, tea strainers . . . infantility . . . I was in those digs and this woman was Meg in *The Birthday Party* and there was a fellow staying there, in Eastbourne, on the coast.'

Having found 'the germs' of his plays, though, what follows is not the procedure adopted by a realist writer, which would involve recording and accurately analysing. Instead, as Pinter underlines, what we have is a natural process, independent of his own will. With specific reference to *The Birthday Party*, he has described his task to Peter Wood as follows:

The thing germinated and bred itself. It proceeded according to its own logic. What did I do? I followed the indications, I kept a sharp eye on the clues I found myself dropping. The writing arranged itself with no trouble into dramatic terms. The characters sounded in my ears – it was apparent to me what one would say and what would be the other's response, at any given point . . . I interfered with them only on a technical level. My task was not to damage their consistency at any time through any external notion of my own.

The emphasis here is on a play which comes to life, a play which has 'germinated and bred itself', without its author's full understanding. Pinter, like Pirandello, for example, believes his characters have their own independent existence. While he admits to interfering with them 'on a technical level', he shows deep respect for their way of being and the mystery surrounding their existence, and in turn he expects his readers, spectators and critics to do the same. And a knowledge of Pinter's creative method helps readers and spectators to understand his characters better, and to accept them on their own terms, even if this entails tolerating bafflement and apparent inconsistencies.

LANGUAGE AND SILENCE

Reality as 'a quicksand', then, and the artistic process evolving independently of the artist's will combine to put a writer in a position not of omnipotence but rather of impotence (in Samuel Beckett's terms, 'a non-knower' or a 'noncanner'). This quicksand of reality and the opaqueness of human nature have, moreover, serious consequences for language. As Pinter said in *Plays: One*:

I have mixed feelings about words myself. Moving among them, sorting them out, watching them appear on the page, from this I derive a considerable pleasure. But at the same time I have another strong feeling about words which amounts to nothing less than nausea. Such a weight of words confronts us day in, day out . . . the bulk of it a stale, dead terminology.

While acknowledging the 'considerable pleasure' he gains from using words in the first part of this statement, Pinter is at the same time troubled. His dismay doubtless stems from a belief that language is an inadequate tool for expressing the persistent flux of reality, is unable to capture the evanesence of life that he and other twentieth-century writers realize refuses to be pinned down on the page.

It is particularly in the area of language that Pinter belongs to our post-modern era. Unlike many other British play-wrights of his generation who shared a similar sort of realism – in his play *Roots*, Arnold Wesker has his character Beatie say: 'Well, language is words . . . it's bridges, so that you can get safely from one place to another' – Pinter, like Beckett and Tom Stoppard, questions the value of language and its ability to express and communicate human experience.

Going hand in hand with his distrust of language is Pinter's reappraisal of silence. In *Plays: One* he has tellingly said: 'The more acute the experience the less articulate [is] its expression.'

This statement points to the inadequacy of words when complex feelings are at stake. More than novels or poetry, plays are a particularly suitable vehicle for experimenting with silence, since theatre communicates through the very presence of the actor on the stage, through scenery and through lighting. Playwrights in a long line from Maeterlinck on, through to Samuel Beckett and Pinter, have succeeded in forging a new and powerful dramatic language out of silence.

DRAMATIC DIALOGUE, SUBTEXT AND SILENT ACTION

On one level, Pinter's dramatic dialogue is extremely realistic, especially in his early works. In *The Room*, *The Dumb Waiter*, *The Birthday Party* and *The Caretaker*, the characters' language is recognizably that of the working class or lower middle class in southern England in the 1950s and 1960s.

In *The Birthday Party* each character has his or her own way of speaking. Goldberg's language is characterized by highly specific Jewish speech rhythms, Jewish colloquial expressions ('Do yourself a favour', see note to page 57) and specific vocabulary to do with Jewish culture like 'Mazoltov' and 'Simchahs' (see notes to page 86) colour his speech. On occasion his language is vulgar and violent: 'Your skin's crabby, you need a shave, your eyes are full of muck, your mouth is like a boghouse . . .' (page 75), and later he complains to Stanley, 'You're beginning to get on my breasts' (page 76). While McCann does not speak a specifically Irish English (Pinter has been careful not to make him a stage Irishman), in performance the role has been played with an Irish accent and sometimes by an Irish actor (Patrick Magee played McCann in the 1964 Aldwych Theatre production). He makes frequent allusions to Irish culture and history. As soon as he meets Stanley, he sings the Irish song 'The Mountains of Morne' and, during the party he entertains the others with the Irish ballad 'The Garden of Eden'. In the interrogation scene he makes numerous references to things Irish: the martyr Oliver Plunkett, the Black and Tans, Drogheda, etc.

Meg, Petey and Lulu speak a lower-middle-class to working-class English. Their language is sometimes characterized by interrogatives without an auxiliary, such as Meg's 'You got your paper?' (Have you got your paper?) and abbreviated forms of compound tenses like 'you got' (you have got) or 'I tell you what' (I'll tell you what). At other times the subject of the verb may be omitted: 'Looked quite nice to me' or 'Been here long?' They sometimes use colloquial expressions: for example, Lulu's 'It's all stuffy in here' and 'Ta-ta, Mrs Boles.' Meg's language is particularly restricted and repetitious, since she qualifies nearly everything with the adjective 'nice'. Stanley's language is the most creative of the four of them, with expressions like 'You succulent old washing bag' (page 48), 'I'd rather have you than a cold in the nose any day' (page 49) and 'Someone's taking the Michael' (page 51); and the most vulgar at times, with 'I bloody well didn't' (page 46) and 'I can't drink this muck' (page 48).

Yet even in Pinter's early works the language is only apparently realistic: it is, in fact, carefully stylized and patterned not just to communicate through its referential meaning but also through a rich subtext. In other words, as well as what a character seems to be saying, another discourse is implied. In a much-quoted statement of 1962 in *Plays: One*, Pinter puts the matter succinctly: 'A language, I repeat, where under what is said, another thing is being said ... One way of looking at speech is to say that it is a constant stratagem to cover nakedness.'

On one level, then, language in Pinter's plays possesses what Austin Quigley has called 'an interrelational function': that is, the characters do not use language exclusively to express and exchange ideas, or to give information about reality. The linguistic exchanges actually show them engaged in a process of establishing and negotiating their relationships. These negotiations, which often take place behind or beyond the words, can be extremely violent. A good example is the interrogation scene as Goldberg and McCann proceed in their attempt to break Stanley down (page 113):

MCCANN. Let you use the club bar.

GOLDBERG. Keep a table reserved.

MCCANN. Help you acknowledge the fast days.

GOLDBERG. Bake you cakes.

MCCANN. Help you kneel on kneeling days.

Through the style and fast-moving rhythm of their patter more than the actual meaning of what they are saying,
the two make it clear to Stanley that they intend to exert
absolute control over him.

Pinter's language can also reflect the elusiveness of
human nature, saying something about man's place in the
world. While the silences and pauses in his plays may seem
to point to the inability of characters to communicate with
one another, Pinter denied this in 1962, in *Plays: One*: I
believe the contrary, I think that we communicate only too
well, in our silence, in what is unsaid, and that what takes
place is a continual evasion, desperate rearguard attempts
to keep ourselves to ourselves.'

So, when one reads or watches a Pinter play, one should
pay attention not only to the content of what is being said
but also to the punctuation marks and the silences which
mark a character's speech. These can work like musical
notation. In the following passage, for instance, Goldberg's
normally uninterrupted speech patterns break down when
Petey pointedly questions him about Stanley's health.
While Goldberg does not admit to Petey that he is feeling
uneasy, the frequent pauses betray his anguish and emo-
tional involvement in Stanley's present state (page 101):

GOLDBERG (*a little uncertainly*). Oh . . . a little better, I
think, a little better. Of course, I'm not really
qualified to say, Mr Boles. I mean, I haven't got the
. . . the qualifications. The best thing would be if
someone with the proper . . . mnn . . . qualifications

... was to have a look at him. Someone with a few letters after his name.

ACTION WITHOUT WORDS

As well as pauses and silences within dialogues, entire mimed sequences stand central to Pinter's plays. In *The Birthday Party* during the game of blind-man's buff at the party, tension gradually increases and the climax is reached through action without words. At such moments Pinter's stage directions are extremely precise as to the exact position of characters onstage and their movement, so creating a vivid moving picture which evolves silently except for two carefully placed exclamations (pages 93–4).

> STANLEY *stands blindfold.* MCCANN *backs slowly across the stage to the left. He breaks* STANLEY'S *glasses, snapping the frames.* MEG *is downstage, left,* LULU *and* GOLDBERG *upstage centre, close together.* STANLEY *begins to move, very slowly, across the stage to the left.* MCCANN *picks up the drum and places it sideways in* STANLEY'S *path.* STANLEY *walks into the drum and falls over with his foot caught in it.*
>
> MEG. Ooh!
>
> GOLDBERG. Sssh!
>
> STANLEY *rises. He begins to move towards* MEG, *dragging the drum on his foot. He reaches her and stops. His hands move towards her and they reach her throat. He begins to strangle her.* MCCANN *and* GOLDBERG *rush forward and throw him off.*

HUMOUR IN PINTER

Pinter employs a wide range of linguistic and stylistic devises to create laughter. In *The Birthday Party*, for example, he has Meg repeat the adjective 'nice' so relentlessly, whatever she is describing, that by the end the audience is poised, waiting for the word's next appearance. Repetition, then, is one device.

Words may also be used in an unusual semantic field (context), once again causing laughter. Stanley tells Meg that his fried bread is 'succulent'. In everyday usage succulent would generally qualify a juicy piece of meat or roast duck, not fried bread. Succulent also possesses sexual overtones and Meg seizes upon this *ambiguity*, asking Stanley if he finds her succulent (sexually attractive). Here comedy derives from the clash between the appearance of this sixty-year-old landlady and the adjective she would like to hear applied to herself.

Pinter's characters sometimes mix linguistic registers, thus producing comic effects. Lulu's choice of 'ta-ta' suggests her working-class origins. She quickly, however, switches momentarily to a middle-class phrase, 'Well, that's a charming proposal', making the audience laugh since the expression seems out of character.

On other occasions, language seems to take hold of the characters, following rapidly and uninterruptedly, while the meaning verges on the absurd. As Goldberg and McCann proceed to interrogate Stanley, both their questions and his answers sometimes seem ridiculous page 78):

GOLDBERG. Why did you stay?
STANLEY. I had a headache!
GOLDBERG. Did you take anything for it?
STANLEY. Yes.
GOLDBERG. What?
STANLEY. Fruit salts!
GOLDBERG. Enos or Andrews?
STANLEY. En – An –
GOLDBERG. Did you stir properly? Did they fizz?

Quick associations link the questions and answers, leading the interrogation nowhere. The participants seem to be merely playing with a kind of language which is familiar to a British audience through television commercials (Enos and Andrews are two brands of liver salts).

Pinter: Playwright, Actor, Director and Screenplay Writer

Pinter's work in a variety of fields has deeply influenced his dramatic writing, because the skills involved in the different roles have proved mutually beneficial. It is not by chance, one feels, that many of his characters are born actors and entertainers. Take McCann, who upon meeting Stanley immediately starts singing an Irish song, which soon turns into a kind of musical duet involving Stanley. The stage directions read: 'STANLEY *joins* MCCANN *in whistling 'The Mountains of Morne'. During the next five lines the whistling is continuous, one whistling while the other speaks, and both whistling together*' (page 68). As Stanley fantasizes to Meg about the wonderful new contract he has just signed, he is transformed into an actor playing the new and highly improbable role of a successful musician.

Pinter's long experience as an actor (and a director) makes him acutely aware of what his characters are doing at any one time, of where they are positioned on the stage. This is particularly noticeable in the stage directions, which are concise, guiding the actor to communicate through his or her actions and gestures. For example, in the blind-man's buff scene, the directions are calculated to create an atmosphere of mounting tension. On other occasions they work to evoke comic effects. The unusual build-up to Lulu's arrival onstage is stipulated carefully:

'*A sudden knock on the door.* LULU'*s voice: Ooh-oo!* MEG *edges past* STANLEY *and collects her shopping bag.* MEG *goes out.* STANLEY *slides to the door and listens*' (page 54). A conversation, alluding to a mysterious 'it' full of comic potential, continues between Meg and Lulu (at this stage nothing more than an unnamed voice) outside, with their voices reaching Stanley and the audience through the letter box (page 54):

> VOICE (*through letter box*). Hullo, Mrs Boles . . .
> MEG. Oh, has it come?
> VOICE. Yes, it's just come.
> MEG. What, is that it?
> VOICE. Yes. I thought I'd bring it round.
> MEG. Is it nice?
> VOICE. Very nice. What shall I do with it.

According to actors who have played Pinter roles, his dramatic language is always very speakable. According to John and Anthea Lahr, Paul Rogers, who played in *The Homecoming* was full of praise.

> Everything in *The Homecoming* was tried and tested before we got it: everything was utterly speakable. There is not a single line which had to be cut to make it speakable. This is an actor's instinct. Ordinarily you have to cut many things which will not fall off the tongue. In Pinter the words really do come off the tongue and teeth beautifully.

Pinter's writing of screenplays has also been important for his stage plays. As well as being a talented 'wordman', he possesses a sensitive eye for the visual – something which has developed through his work in film. As early as *The Birthday Party*, in, for example, the blind-man's buff scene, there are strong and carefully designed stage-pictures.

During Act Two, moreover, Pinter uses the technique of blackout rather than a division into scenes to give the act its particular structure.

Later the reliance on film techniques in his stage plays increased and in *The Caretaker* (1960) it is already more noticeable. Here the traditional curtain of *The Birthday Party* which divided each act has disappeared and the play is divided by blackouts and fades, reflecting a fusion of cinema and theatrical techniques.

PINTER'S TRAGICOMEDY AND AUDIENCE RECEPTION

Tragicomedy is characteristic of much modern drama (Beckett subtitled *Waiting for Godot* 'a tragicomedy in two acts'). The present-day usage of the term implies not tragic scenes alternating with comic ones, but rather, to quote George Bernard Shaw, 'a chemical combination which [makes] the spectator laugh with one side of his mouth and cry with the other'.

Pinter's early plays such as *The Birthday Party* and *The Caretaker*, can be defined as tragicomic. While Pinter presents us with a bleak vision of the human condition in so far as his characters invariably live in a world where love and even affection are missing, and they are generally without religious faith or ideals, at the same time they cannot be said to be purely tragic figures.

In *The Birthday Party* the interrogation scene is tragicomic. On the one hand, the style of interrogation is frightening and disturbing; on the other, it is reminiscent of old-fashioned music-hall patter and today's stand-up comedians. In performance, then, one laughs at the nonsensical sequence of accusations, including well-known jokes like 'Why did the chicken cross the road?', and the couple's inventions of absurd associations of ideas. But at the same time, one feels an underlying and mounting sense of anguish, since from early on in the play Stanley has shown his deep concern at hearing about the two men who are expected to arrive.

The Birthday Party

The Birthday Party was first presented by Michael Codron and David Hall at the Arts Theatre, Cambridge, on 28 April 1958, and subsequently at the Lyric Opera House, Hammersmith, with the following cast:

PETEY	Willoughby Gray
MEG	Beatrix Lehmann
STANLEY	Richard Pearson
LULU	Wendy Hutchinson
GOLDBERG	John Slater
MCCANN	John Stratton

Directed by Peter Wood

The Birthday Party was revived by the Royal Shakespeare Company at the Aldwych Theatre, London, on 18 June 1964 with the following cast:

PETEY	Newton Blick
MEG	Doris Hare
STANLEY	Bryan Pringle
LULU	Janet Suzman
GOLDBERG	Brewster Mason
MCCANN	Patrick Magee

Directed by Harold Pinter

The Birthday Party was broadcast on BBC Television on 28 June 1987 with the following cast:

PETEY	Robert Lang
MEG	Joan Plowright
STANLEY	Kenneth Cranham
LULU	Julie Walters
GOLDBERG	Harold Pinter
MCCANN	Colin Blakely

Directed by Kenneth Ives

ACT I A morning in summer
ACT II Evening of the same day
ACT III The next morning

Characters

PETEY, *a man in his sixties*
MEG, *a woman in her sixties*
STANLEY, *a man in his late thirties*
LULU, *a girl in her twenties*
GOLDBERG, *a man in his fifties*
MCCANN, *a man of thirty*

Act One

The living-room of a house in a seaside town. A door leading to the hall down left. Back door and small window up left. Kitchen hatch, centre back. Kitchen door up right. Table and chairs, centre.

PETEY enters from the door on the left with a paper and sits at the table. He begins to read. MEG'S voice comes through the kitchen hatch.

MEG. Is that you, Petey?

> *Pause.*

Petey, is that you?

> *Pause.*

Petey?
PETEY. What?
MEG. Is that you?
PETEY. Yes, it's me.
MEG. What? (*Her face appears at the hatch.*) Are you back?
PETEY. Yes.
MEG. I've got your cornflakes ready. (*She disappears and re-appears.*) Here's your cornflakes.

> *He rises and takes the plate from her, sits at the table, props up the paper and begins to eat. MEG enters by the kitchen door.*

Are they nice?
PETEY. Very nice.
MEG. I thought they'd be nice. (*She sits at the table.*) You got your paper?
PETEY. Yes.

MEG. Is it good?

PETEY. Not bad.

MEG. What does it say?

PETEY. Nothing much.

MEG. You read me out some nice bits yesterday.

PETEY. Yes, well, I haven't finished this one yet.

MEG. Will you tell me when you come to something good?

PETEY. Yes.

> *Pause.*

MEG. Have you been working hard this morning?

PETEY. No. Just stacked a few of the old chairs. Cleaned up a
bit.

MEG. Is it nice out?

PETEY. Very nice.

> *Pause.*

MEG. Is Stanley up yet?

PETEY. I don't know. Is he?

MEG. I don't know. I haven't seen him down yet.

PETEY. Well then, he can't be up.

MEG. Haven't you seen him down?

PETEY. I've only just come in.

MEG. He must be still asleep.

> *She looks round the room, stands, goes to the sideboard and
> takes a pair of socks from a drawer, collects wool and a needle
> and goes back to the table.*

What time did you go out this morning, Petey?

PETEY. Same time as usual.

MEG. Was it dark?

PETEY. No, it was light.

MEG (*beginning to darn*). But sometimes you go out in the
morning and it's dark.

PETEY. That's in the winter.

MEG. Oh, in winter.

PETEY. Yes, it gets light later in winter.

MEG. Oh.

Pause.

What are you reading?

PETEY. Someone's just had a baby.

MEG. Oh, they haven't! Who?

PETEY. Some girl.

MEG. Who, Petey, who?

PETEY. I don't think you'd know her.

MEG. What's her name?

PETEY. Lady Mary Splatt.

MEG. I don't know her.

PETEY. No.

MEG. What is it?

PETEY (*studying the paper*). Er—a girl.

MEG. Not a boy?

PETEY. No.

MEG. Oh, what a shame. I'd be sorry. I'd much rather have a little boy.

PETEY. A little girl's all right.

MEG. I'd much rather have a little boy.

Pause.

PETEY. I've finished my cornflakes.

MEG. Were they nice?

PETEY. Very nice.

MEG. I've got something else for you.

PETEY. Good.

She rises, takes his plate and exits into the kitchen. She then appears at the hatch with two pieces of fried bread on a plate.

MEG. Here you are, Petey.

He rises, collects the plate, looks at it, sits at the table. MEG *re-enters.*

Is it nice?

PETEY. I haven't tasted it yet.

MEG. I bet you don't know what it is.

PETEY. Yes, I do.

MEG. What is it, then?

PETEY. Fried bread.

MEG. That's right.

> *He begins to eat.*
> *She watches him eat.*

PETEY. Very nice.

MEG. I knew it was.

PETEY (*turning to her*). Oh, Meg, two men came up to me on the beach last night.

MEG. Two men?

PETEY. Yes. They wanted to know if we could put them up for a couple of nights.

MEG. Put them up? Here?

PETEY. Yes.

MEG. How many men?

PETEY. Two.

MEG. What did you say?

PETEY. Well, I said I didn't know. So they said they'd come round to find out.

MEG. Are they coming?

PETEY. Well, they said they would.

MEG. Had they heard about us, Petey?

PETEY. They must have done.

MEG. Yes, they must have done. They must have heard this was a very good boarding house. It is. This house is on the list.

PETEY. It is.

MEG. I know it is.

PETEY. They might turn up today. Can you do it?

MEG. Oh, I've got that lovely room they can have.

PETEY. You've got a room ready?

MEG. I've got the room with the armchair all ready for visitors.

PETEY. You're sure?

MEG. Yes, that'll be all right then, if they come today.

PETEY. Good.

She takes the socks etc. back to the sideboard drawer.

MEG. I'm going to wake that boy.

PETEY. There's a new show coming to the Palace.

MEG. On the pier?

PETEY. No. The Palace, in the town.

MEG. Stanley could have been in it, if it was on the pier.

PETEY. This is a straight show.

MEG. What do you mean?

PETEY. No dancing or singing.

MEG. What do they do then?

PETEY. They just talk.

Pause.

MEG. Oh.

PETEY. You like a song eh, Meg?

MEG. I like listening to the piano. I used to like watching Stanley play the piano. Of course, he didn't sing. (*Looking at the door.*) I'm going to call that boy.

PETEY. Didn't you take him up his cup of tea?

MEG. I always take him up his cup of tea. But that was a long time ago.

PETEY. Did he drink it?

MEG. I made him. I stood there till he did. I'm going to call him. (*She goes to the door.*) Stan! Stanny! (*She listens.*) Stan! I'm coming up to fetch you if you don't come down! I'm coming up! I'm going to count three! One! Two! Three! I'm coming to get you! (*She exits and goes upstairs. In a moment, shouts from* STANLEY, *wild laughter from* MEG. PETEY *takes his plate to the hatch. Shouts. Laughter.*

PETEY *sits at the table. Silence. She returns.*) He's coming down. (*She is panting and arranges her hair.*) I told him if he didn't hurry up he'd get no breakfast.

PETEY. That did it, eh?

MEG. I'll get his cornflakes.

> MEG *exits to the kitchen.* PETEY *reads the paper.* STANLEY *enters. He is unshaven, in his pyjama jacket and wears glasses. He sits at the table.*

PETEY. Morning, Stanley.

STANLEY. Morning.

> *Silence.* MEG *enters with the bowl of cornflakes, which she sets on the table.*

MEG. So he's come down at last, has he? He's come down at last for his breakfast. But he doesn't deserve any, does he, Petey? (STANLEY *stares at the cornflakes.*) Did you sleep well?

STANLEY. I didn't sleep at all.

MEG. You didn't sleep at all? Did you hear that, Petey? Too tired to eat your breakfast, I suppose? Now you eat up those cornflakes like a good boy. Go on.

> *He begins to eat.*

STANLEY. What's it like out today?

PETEY. Very nice.

STANLEY. Warm?

PETEY. Well, there's a good breeze blowing.

STANLEY. Cold?

PETEY. No, no, I wouldn't say it was cold.

MEG. What are the cornflakes like, Stan?

STANLEY. Horrible.

MEG. Those flakes? Those lovely flakes? You're a liar, a little liar. They're refreshing. It says so. For people when they get up late.

STANLEY. The milk's off.

MEG. It's not. Petey ate his, didn't you, Petey?

PETEY. That's right.

MEG. There you are then.

STANLEY. All right, I'll go on to the second course.

MEG. He hasn't finished the first course and he wants to go on to the second course!

STANLEY. I feel like something cooked.

MEG. Well, I'm not going to give it to you.

PETEY. Give it to him.

MEG (*sitting at the table, right*). I'm not going to.

Pause.

STANLEY. No breakfast.

Pause.

All night long I've been dreaming about this breakfast.

MEG. I thought you said you didn't sleep.

STANLEY. Day-dreaming. All night long. And now she won't give me any. Not even a crust of bread on the table.

Pause.

Well, I can see I'll have to go down to one of those smart hotels on the front.

MEG (*rising quickly*). You won't get a better breakfast there than here.

She exits to the kitchen. STANLEY *yawns broadly.* MEG *appears at the hatch with a plate.*

Here you are. You'll like this.

PETEY *rises, collects the plate, brings it to the table, puts it in front of* STANLEY, *and sits.*

STANLEY. What's this?

PETEY. Fried bread.

MEG (*entering*). Well, I bet you don't know what it is.

STANLEY. Oh yes I do.

MEG. What?

STANLEY. Fried bread.

MEG. He knew.

STANLEY. What a wonderful surprise.

MEG. You didn't expect that, did you?

STANLEY. I bloody well didn't.

PETEY (*rising*). Well, I'm off.

MEG. You going back to work?

PETEY. Yes.

MEG. Your tea! You haven't had your tea!

PETEY. That's all right. No time now.

MEG. I've got it made inside.

PETEY. No, never mind. See you later. Ta-ta, Stan.

STANLEY. Ta-ta.

PETEY *exits, left.*

Tch, tch, tch, tch.

MEG (*defensively*). What do you mean?

STANLEY. You're a bad wife.

MEG. I'm not. Who said I am?

STANLEY. Not to make your husband a cup of tea. Terrible.

MEG. He knows I'm not a bad wife.

STANLEY. Giving him sour milk instead.

MEG. It wasn't sour.

STANLEY. Disgraceful.

MEG. You mind your own business, anyway. (STANLEY *eats.*) You won't find many better wives than me, I can tell you. I keep a very nice house and I keep it clean.

STANLEY. Whoo!

MEG. Yes! And this house is very well known, for a very good boarding house for visitors.

STANLEY. Visitors? Do you know how many visitors you've had since I've been here?

MEG. How many?

STANLEY. One.

MEG. Who?

STANLEY. Me! I'm your visitor.

MEG. You're a liar. This house is on the list.

STANLEY. I bet it is.

MEG. I know it is.

He pushes his plate away and picks up the paper.

Was it nice?

STANLEY. What?

MEG. The fried bread.

STANLEY. Succulent.

MEG. You shouldn't say that word.

STANLEY. What word?

MEG. That word you said.

STANLEY. What, succulent—?

MEG. Don't say it!

STANLEY. What's the matter with it?

MEG. You shouldn't say that word to a married woman.

STANLEY. Is that a fact?

MEG. Yes.

STANLEY. Well, I never knew that.

MEG. Well, it's true.

STANLEY. Who told you that?

MEG. Never you mind.

STANLEY. Well, if I can't say it to a married woman who can I say it to?

MEG. You're bad.

STANLEY. What about some tea?

MEG. Do you want some tea? (STANLEY *reads the paper.*) Say please.

STANLEY. Please.

MEG. Say sorry first.

STANLEY. Sorry first.

MEG. No. Just sorry.

STANLEY. Just sorry!

MEG. You deserve the strap.

STANLEY. Don't do that!

> *She takes his plate and ruffles his hair as she passes.*
> STANLEY *exclaims and throws her arm away. She goes into*
> *the kitchen. He rubs his eyes under his glasses and picks up*
> *the paper. She enters.*

I brought the pot in.

STANLEY (*absently*). I don't know what I'd do without you.

MEG. You don't deserve it though.

STANLEY. Why not?

MEG (*pouring the tea, coyly*). Go on. Calling me that.

STANLEY. How long has that tea been in the pot?

MEG. It's good tea. Good strong tea.

STANLEY. This isn't tea. It's gravy!

MEG. It's not.

STANLEY. Get out of it. You succulent old washing bag.

MEG. I am not! And it isn't your place to tell me if I am!

STANLEY. And it isn't your place to come into a man's bed-
room and—wake him up.

MEG. Stanny! Don't you like your cup of tea of a morning—
the one I bring you?

STANLEY. I can't drink this muck. Didn't anyone ever tell you
to warm the pot, at least?

MEG. That's good strong tea, that's all.

STANLEY (*putting his head in his hands*). Oh God, I'm tired.

> *Silence.* MEG *goes to the sideboard, collects a duster, and*
> *vaguely dusts the room, watching him. She comes to the*
> *table and dusts it.*

Not the bloody table!

> *Pause.*

MEG. Stan?

STANLEY. What?

MEG (*shyly*). Am I really succulent?

STANLEY. Oh, you are. I'd rather have you than a cold in the nose any day.

MEG. You're just saying that.

STANLEY (*violently*). Look, why don't you get this place cleared up! It's a pigsty. And another thing, what about my room? It needs sweeping. It needs papering. I need a new room!

MEG (*sensual, stroking his arm*). Oh, Stan, that's a lovely room. I've had some lovely afternoons in that room.

> *He recoils from her hand in disgust, stands and exits quickly by the door on the left. She collects his cup and the teapot and takes them to the hatch shelf. The street door slams.* STANLEY *returns.*

MEG. Is the sun shining? (*He crosses to the window, takes a cigarette and matches from his pyjama jacket, and lights his cigarette.*) What are you smoking?

STANLEY. A cigarette.

MEG. Are you going to give me one?

STANLEY. No.

MEG. I like cigarettes. (*He stands at the window, smoking. She crosses behind him and tickles the back of his neck.*) Tickle, tickle.

STANLEY (*pushing her*). Get away from me.

MEG. Are you going out?

STANLEY. Not with you.

MEG. But I'm going shopping in a minute.

STANLEY. Go.

MEG. You'll be lonely, all by yourself.

STANLEY. Will I?

MEG. Without your old Meg. I've got to get things in for the two gentlemen.

A pause. STANLEY *slowly raises his head. He speaks without turning.*

STANLEY. What two gentlemen?

MEG. I'm expecting visitors.

He turns.

STANLEY. What?

MEG. You didn't know that, did you?

STANLEY. What are you talking about?

MEG. Two gentlemen asked Petey if they could come and stay for a couple of nights. I'm expecting them. (*She picks up the duster and begins to wipe the cloth on the table.*)

STANLEY. I don't believe it.

MEG. It's true.

STANLEY (*moving to her*). You're saying it on purpose.

MEG. Petey told me this morning.

STANLEY (*grinding his cigarette*). When was this? When did he see them?

MEG. Last night.

STANLEY. Who are they?

MEG. I don't know.

STANLEY. Didn't he tell you their names?

MEG. No.

STANLEY (*pacing the room*). Here? They wanted to come here?

MEG. Yes, they did. (*She takes the curlers out of her hair.*)

STANLEY. Why?

MEG. This house is on the list.

STANLEY. But who are they?

MEG. You'll see when they come.

STANLEY (*decisively*). They won't come.

MEG. Why not?

STANLEY (*quickly*). I tell you they won't come. Why didn't they come last night, if they were coming?

MEG. Perhaps they couldn't find the place in the dark. It's not easy to find in the dark.

STANLEY. They won't come. Someone's taking the Michael. Forget all about it. It's a false alarm. A false alarm. (*He sits at the table.*) Where's my tea?

MEG. I took it away. You didn't want it.

STANLEY. What do you mean, you took it away?

MEG. I took it away.

STANLEY. What did you take it away for?

MEG. You didn't want it!

STANLEY. Who said I didn't want it?

MEG. You did!

STANLEY. Who gave you the right to take away my tea?

MEG. You wouldn't drink it.

STANLEY *stares at her.*

STANLEY (*quietly*). Who do you think you're talking to?

MEG (*uncertainly*). What?

STANLEY. Come here.

MEG. What do you mean?

STANLEY. Come over here.

MEG. No.

STANLEY. I want to ask you something. (MEG *fidgets nervously. She does not go to him.*) Come on. (*Pause.*) All right. I can ask it from here just as well. (*Deliberately.*) Tell me, Mrs Boles, when you address yourself to me, do you ever ask yourself who exactly you are talking to? Eh?

Silence. He groans, his trunk falls forward, his head falls into his hands.

MEG (*in a small voice*). Didn't you enjoy your breakfast, Stan? (*She approaches the table.*) Stan? When are you going to play the piano again? (STANLEY *grunts.*) Like you used to? (STANLEY *grunts.*) I used to like watching you play the piano. When are you going to play it again?

STANLEY. I can't, can I?

MEG. Why not?

STANLEY. I haven't got a piano, have I?

MEG. No, I meant like when you were working. That piano.

STANLEY. Go and do your shopping.

MEG. But you wouldn't have to go away if you got a job, would you? You could play the piano on the pier.

He looks at her, then speaks airily.

STANLEY. I've . . . er . . . I've been offered a job, as a matter of fact.

MEG. What?

STANLEY. Yes. I'm considering a job at the moment.

MEG. You're not.

STANLEY. A good one, too. A night club. In Berlin.

MEG. Berlin?

STANLEY. Berlin. A night club. Playing the piano. A fabulous salary. And all found.

MEG. How long for?

STANLEY. We don't stay in Berlin. Then we go to Athens.

MEG. How long for?

STANLEY. Yes. Then we pay a flying visit to . . . er . . . whatsisname. . . .

MEG. Where?

STANLEY. Constantinople. Zagreb. Vladivostock. It's a round the world tour.

MEG (*sitting at the table*). Have you played the piano in those places before?

STANLEY. Played the piano? I've played the piano all over the world. All over the country. (*Pause.*) I once gave a concert.

MEG. A concert?

STANLEY (*reflectively*). Yes. It was a good one, too. They were all there that night. Every single one of them. It was a great success. Yes. A concert. At Lower Edmonton.

MEG. What did you wear?

STANLEY (*to himself*). I had a unique touch. Absolutely unique. They came up to me. They came up to me and said they

were grateful. Champagne we had that night, the lot. (*Pause.*)
My father nearly came down to hear me. Well, I dropped
him a card anyway. But I don't think he could make it. No,
I—I lost the address, that was it. (*Pause.*) Yes. Lower Edmonton. Then after that, you know what they did? They
carved me up. Carved me up. It was all arranged, it was all
worked out. My next concert. Somewhere else it was. In
winter. I went down there to play. Then, when I got there,
the hall was closed, the place was shuttered up, not even a
caretaker. They'd locked it up. (*Takes off his glasses and
wipes them on his pyjama jacket.*) A fast one. They pulled a
fast one. I'd like to know who was responsible for that.
(*Bitterly.*) All right, Jack, I can take a tip. They want me to
crawl down on my bended knees. Well I can take a tip . . .
any day of the week. (*He replaces his glasses, then looks at
MEG.*) Look at her. You're just an old piece of rock cake,
aren't you? (*He rises and leans across the table to her.*) That's
what you are, aren't you?

MEG. Don't you go away again, Stan. You stay here. You'll
be better off. You stay with your old Meg. (*He groans and
lies across the table.*) Aren't you feeling well this morning,
Stan. Did you pay a visit this morning?

*He stiffens, then lifts himself slowly, turns to face her and
speaks lightly, casually.*

STANLEY. Meg. Do you know what?
MEG. What?
STANLEY. Have you heard the latest?
MEG. No.
STANLEY. I'll bet you have.
MEG. I haven't.
STANLEY. Shall I tell you?
MEG. What latest?
STANLEY. You haven't heard it?
MEG. No.

STANLEY (*advancing*). They're coming today. They're coming in a van.

MEG. Who?

STANLEY. And do you know what they've got in that van?

MEG. What?

STANLEY. They've got a wheelbarrow in that van.

MEG (*breathlessly*). They haven't.

STANLEY. Oh yes they have.

MEG. You're a liar.

STANLEY (*advancing upon her*). A big wheelbarrow. And when the van stops they wheel it out, and they wheel it up the garden path, and then they knock at the front door.

MEG. They don't.

STANLEY. They're looking for someone.

MEG. They're not.

STANLEY. They're looking for someone. A certain person.

MEG (*hoarsely*). No, they're not!

STANLEY. Shall I tell you who they're looking for?

MEG. No!

STANLEY. You don't want me to tell you?

MEG. You're a liar!

A sudden knock on the front door. LULU'S *voice: Ooh-ooh!*
MEG *edges past* STANLEY *and collects her shopping bag.*
MEG *goes out.* STANLEY *sidles to the door and listens.*

VOICE (*through letter box*). Hullo, Mrs Boles . . .

MEG. Oh, has it come?

VOICE. Yes, it's just come.

MEG. What, is that it?

VOICE. Yes. I thought I'd bring it round.

MEG. Is it nice?

VOICE. Very nice. What shall I do with it?

MEG. Well, I don't . . . (*Whispers.*)

VOICE. No, of course not . . .(*Whispers.*)

MEG. All right, but . . . (*Whispers.*)

VOICE. I won't . . . (*Whispers.*) Ta-ta, Mrs Boles.

STANLEY *quickly sits at the table. Enter* LULU.

LULU. Oh, hullo.

STANLEY. Ay-ay.

LULU. I just want to leave this in here.

STANLEY. Do. (LULU *crosses to the sideboard and puts a solid, round parcel upon it.*) That's a bulky object.

LULU. You're not to touch it.

STANLEY. Why would I want to touch it?

LULU. Well, you're not to, anyway.

LULU *walks upstage.*

LULU. Why don't you open the door? It's all stuffy in here.

She opens the back door.

STANLEY (*rising*): Stuffy? I disinfected the place this morning.

LULU (*at the door*). Oh, that's better.

STANLEY. I think it's going to rain to-day. What do you think?

LULU. I hope so. You could do with it.

STANLEY. Me! I was in the sea at half past six.

LULU. Were you?

STANLEY. I went right out to the headland and back before breakfast. Don't you believe me!

She sits, takes out a compact and powders her nose.

LULU (*offering him the compact*). Do you want to have a look at your face? (STANLEY *withdraws from the table.*) You could do with a shave, do you know that? (STANLEY *sits, right at the table.*) Don't you ever go out? (*He does not answer.*) I mean, what do you do, just sit around the house like this all day long? (*Pause.*) Hasn't Mrs Boles got enough to do without having you under her feet all day long?

STANLEY. I always stand on the table when she sweeps the
   floor.

LULU. Why don't you have a wash? You look terrible.

STANLEY. A wash wouldn't make any difference.

LULU (*rising*). Come out and get a bit of air. You depress me,
   looking like that.

STANLEY. Air? Oh, I don't know about that.

LULU. It's lovely out. And I've got a few sandwiches.

STANLEY. What sort of sandwiches?

LULU. Cheese.

STANLEY. I'm a big eater, you know.

LULU. That's all right. I'm not hungry.

STANLEY (*abruptly*). How would you like to go away with
   me?

LULU. Where.

STANLEY. Nowhere. Still, we could go.

LULU. But where could we go?

STANLEY. Nowhere. There's nowhere to go. So we could just
   go. It wouldn't matter.

LULU. We might as well stay here.

STANLEY. No. It's no good here.

LULU. Well, where else is there?

STANLEY. Nowhere.

LULU. Well, that's a charming proposal. (*He gets up.*) Do you
   have to wear those glasses?

STANLEY. Yes.

LULU. So you're not coming out for a walk?

STANLEY. I can't at the moment.

LULU. You're a bit of a washout, aren't you?

> She exits, left. STANLEY stands. He then goes to the mirror
> and looks in it. He goes into the kitchen, takes off his glasses
> and begins to wash his face. A pause. Enter, by the back door,
> GOLDBERG and MCCANN. MCCANN carries two suitcases,
> GOLDBERG a briefcase. They halt inside the door, then

walk downstage. STANLEY, *wiping his face, glimpses their backs through the hatch.* GOLDBERG *and* MCCANN *look round the room.* STANLEY *slips on his glasses, sidles through the kitchen door and out of the back door.*

MCCANN. Is this it?

GOLDBERG. This is it.

MCCANN. Are you sure?

GOLDBERG. Sure I'm sure.

Pause.

MCCANN. What now?

GOLDBERG. Don't worry yourself, McCann. Take a seat.

MCCANN. What about you?

GOLDBERG. What about me?

MCCANN. Are you going to take a seat?

GOLDBERG. We'll both take a seat. (MCCANN *puts down the suitcase and sits at the table, left.*) Sit back, McCann. Relax. What's the matter with you? I bring you down for a few days to the seaside. Take a holiday. Do yourself a favour. Learn to relax, McCann, or you'll never get anywhere.

MCCANN. Ah sure, I do try, Nat.

GOLDBERG (*sitting at the table, right*). The secret is breathing. Take my tip. It's a well-known fact. Breathe in, breathe out, take a chance, let yourself go, what can you lose? Look at me. When I was an apprentice yet, McCann, every second Friday of the month my Uncle Barney used to take me to the seaside, regular as clockwork. Brighton, Canvey Island, Rottingdean—Uncle Barney wasn't particular. After lunch on Shabbuss we'd go and sit in a couple of deck chairs—you know, the ones with canopies—we'd have a little paddle, we'd watch the tide coming in, going out, the sun coming down—golden days, believe me, McCann. (*Reminiscent.*) Uncle Barney. Of course, he was an impeccable dresser. One of the old school. He had a house just outside Basingstoke at the time. Respected by the whole community.

Culture? Don't talk to me about culture. He was an all-round man, what do you mean? He was a cosmopolitan.

MCCANN. Hey, Nat. . . .

GOLDBERG (*reflectively*). Yes. One of the old school.

MCCANN. Nat. How do we know this is the right house?

GOLDBERG. What?

MCCANN. How do we know this is the right house?

GOLDBERG. What makes you think it's the wrong house?

MCCANN. I didn't see a number on the gate.

GOLDBERG. I wasn't looking for a number.

MCCANN. No?

GOLDBERG (*settling in the armchair*). You know one thing Uncle Barney taught me? Uncle Barney taught me that the word of a gentleman is enough. That's why, when I had to go away on business I never carried any money. One of my sons used to come with me. He used to carry a few coppers. For a paper, perhaps, to see how the M.C.C. was getting on overseas. Otherwise my name was good. Besides, I was a very busy man.

MCCANN. What about this, Nat? Isn't it about time someone came in?

GOLDBERG. McCann, what are you so nervous about? Pull yourself together. Everywhere you go these days it's like a funeral.

MCCANN. That's true.

GOLDBERG. True? Of course it's true. It's more than true. It's a fact.

MCCANN. You may be right.

GOLDBERG. What is it, McCann? You don't trust me like you did in the old days?

MCCANN. Sure I trust you, Nat.

GOLDBERG. But why is it that before you do a job you're all over the place, and when you're doing the job you're as cool as a whistle?

MCCANN. I don't know, Nat. I'm just all right once I know what I'm doing. When I know what I'm doing, I'm all right.

GOLDBERG. Well, you do it very well.

MCCANN. Thank you, Nat.

GOLDBERG. You know what I said when this job came up. I mean naturally they approached me to take care of it. And you know who I asked for?

MCCANN. Who?

GOLDBERG. You.

MCCANN. That was very good of you, Nat.

GOLDBERG. No, it was nothing. You're a capable man, McCann.

MCCANN. That's a great compliment, Nat, coming from a man in your position.

GOLDBERG. Well, I've got a position, I won't deny it.

MCCANN. You certainly have.

GOLDBERG. I would never deny that I had a position.

MCCANN. And what a position!

GOLDBERG. It's not a thing I would deny.

MCCANN. Yes, it's true, you've done a lot for me. I appreciate it.

GOLDBERG. Say no more.

MCCANN. You've always been a true Christian.

GOLDBERG. In a way.

MCCANN. No, I just thought I'd tell you that I appreciate it.

GOLDBERG. It's unnecessary to recapitulate.

MCCANN. You're right there.

GOLDBERG. Quite unnecessary.

Pause. MCCANN *leans forward.*

MCCANN. Hey Nat, just one thing. . . .

GOLDBERG. What now?

MCCANN. This job—no, listen—this job, is it going to be like anything we've ever done before?

GOLDBERG. Tch, tch, tch.

MCCANN. No, just tell me that. Just that, and I won't ask any more.

> GOLDBERG *sighs, stands, goes behind the table, ponders, looks at* MCCANN, *and then speaks in a quiet, fluent, official tone.*

GOLDBERG. The main issue is a singular issue and quite distinct from your previous work. Certain elements, however, might well approximate in points of procedure to some of your other activities. All is dependent on the attitude of our subject. At all events, McCann, I can assure you that the assignment will be carried out and the mission accomplished with no excessive aggravation to you or myself. Satisfied?

MCCANN. Sure. Thank you, Nat.

> MEG *enters, left.*

GOLDBERG. Ah, Mrs Boles?

MEG. Yes?

GOLDBERG. We spoke to your husband last night. Perhaps he mentioned us? We heard that you kindly let rooms for gentlemen. So I brought my friend along with me. We were after a nice place, you understand. So we came to you. I'm Mr Goldberg and this is Mr McCann.

MEG. Very pleased to meet you.

> *They shake hands.*

GOLDBERG. We're pleased to meet you, too.

MEG. That's very nice.

GOLDBERG. You're right. How often do you meet someone it's a pleasure to meet?

MCCANN. Never.

GOLDBERG. But today it's different. How are you keeping, Mrs Boles?

MEG. Oh, very well, thank you.

GOLDBERG. Yes? Really?

MEG. Oh yes, really.

GOLDBERG. I'm glad.

> GOLDBERG *sits at the table, right.*

GOLDBERG. Well, so what do you say? You can manage to put us up, eh, Mrs Boles?

MEG. Well, it would have been easier last week.

GOLDBERG. It would, eh?

MEG. Yes.

GOLDBERG. Why? How many have you got here at the moment?

MEG. Just one at the moment.

GOLDBERG. Just one?

MEG. Yes. Just one. Until you came.

GOLDBERG. And your husband, of course?

MEG. Yes, but he sleeps with me.

GOLDBERG. What does he do, your husband?

MEG. He's a deck-chair attendant.

GOLDBERG. Oh, very nice.

MEG. Yes, he's out in all weathers.

> *She begins to take her purchases from her bag.*

GOLDBERG. Of course. And your guest? Is he a man?

MEG. A man?

GOLDBERG. Or a woman?

MEG. No. A man.

GOLDBERG. Been here long?

MEG. He's been here about a year now.

GOLDBERG. Oh yes. A resident. What's his name?

MEG. Stanley Webber.

GOLDBERG. Oh yes? Does he work here?

MEG. He used to work. He used to be a pianist. In a concert party on the pier.

GOLDBERG. Oh yes? On the pier, eh? Does he play a nice piano?

MEG. Oh, lovely. (*She sits at the table.*) He once gave a concert.

GOLDBERG. Oh? Where?

MEG (*falteringly*). In . . . a big hall. His father gave him
champagne. But then they locked the place up and he
couldn't get out. The caretaker had gone home. So he had
to wait until the morning before he could get out. (*With
confidence.*) They were very grateful. (*Pause.*) And then they
all wanted to give him a tip. And so he took the tip. And
then he got a fast train and he came down here.

GOLDBERG. Really?

MEG. Oh yes. Straight down.

> *Pause.*

MEG. I wish he could have played tonight.

GOLDBERG. Why tonight?

MEG. It's his birthday today.

GOLDBERG. His birthday?

MEG. Yes. Today. But I'm not going to tell him until tonight.

GOLDBERG. Doesn't he know it's his birthday?

MEG. He hasn't mentioned it.

GOLDBERG (*thoughtfully*). Ah! Tell me. Are you going to have
a party?

MEG. A party?

GOLDBERG. Weren't you going to have one?

MEG (*her eyes wide*). No.

GOLDBERG. Well, of course, you must have one. (*He stands.*)
We'll have a party, eh? What do you say?

MEG. Oh yes!

GOLDBERG. Sure. We'll give him a party. Leave it to me.

MEG. Oh, that's wonderful, Mr Gold—

GOLDBERG. Berg.

MEG. Berg.

GOLDBERG. You like the idea?

MEG. Oh, I'm so glad you came today.

GOLDBERG. If we hadn't come today we'd have come tomorrow. Still, I'm glad we came today. Just in time for his

birthday.

MEG. I wanted to have a party But you must have people for a
party.

GOLDBERG. And now you've got McCann and me. McCann's
the life and soul of any party.

MCCANN. What?

GOLDBERG. What do you think of that, McCann? There's a
gentleman living here. He's got a birthday today, and he's
forgotten all about it. So we're going to remind him. We're
going to give him a party.

MCCANN. Oh, is that a fact?

MEG. Tonight.

GOLDBERG. Tonight.

MEG. I'll put on my party dress.

GOLDBERG. And I'll get some bottles.

MEG. And I'll invite Lulu this afternoon. Oh, this is going to
cheer Stanley up. It will. He's been down in the dumps lately.

GOLDBERG. We'll bring him out of himself.

MEG. I hope I look nice in my dress.

GOLDBERG. Madam, you'll look like a tulip.

MEG. What colour?

GOLDBERG. Er—well, I'll have to see the dress first.

MCCANN. Could I go up to my room?

MEG. Oh, I've put you both together. Do you mind being both
together?

GOLDBERG. I don't mind. Do you mind, McCann?

MCCANN. No.

MEG. What time shall we have the party?

GOLDBERG. Nine o'clock.

MCCANN (*at the door*). Is this the way?

MEG (*rising*). I'll show you. If you don't mind coming upstairs.

GOLDBERG. With a tulip? It's a pleasure.

> MEG *and* GOLDBERG *exit laughing, followed by* MCCANN.
> STANLEY *appears at the window. He enters by the back*

door. He goes to the door on the left, opens it and listens.
Silence, He walks to the table. He stands. He sits, as MEG
enters. She crosses and hangs her shopping bag on a hook. He
lights a match and watches it burn.

STANLEY. Who is it?

MEG. The two gentlemen.

STANLEY. What two gentlemen?

MEG. The ones that were coming. I just took them to their
room. They were thrilled with their room.

STANLEY. They've come?

MEG. They're very nice, Stan.

STANLEY. Why didn't they come last night?

MEG. They said the beds were wonderful.

STANLEY. Who are they?

MEG (*sitting*). They're very nice, Stanley.

STANLEY. I said, who are they?

MEG. I've told you, the two gentlemen.

STANLEY. I didn't think they'd come.

He rises and walks to the window.

MEG. They have. They were here when I came in.

STANLEY. What do they want here?

MEG. They want to stay.

STANLEY. How long for?

MEG. They didn't say.

STANLEY (*turning*). But why here? Why not somewhere else?

MEG. This house is on the list.

STANLEY (*coming down*). What are they called? What are their
names?

MEG. Oh, Stanley, I can't remember.

STANLEY. They told you, didn't they? Or didn't they tell you?

MEG. Yes, they. . . .

STANLEY. Then what are they? Come on. Try to remember.

MEG. Why, Stan? Do you know them?

STANLEY. How do I know if I know them until I know their names?

MEG. Well . . . he told me, I remember.

STANLEY. Well?

She thinks.

MEG. Gold—something.

STANLEY. Goldsomething?

MEG. Yes. Gold. . . .

STANLEY. Yes?

MEG. Goldberg.

STANLEY. Goldberg?

MEG. That's right. That was one of them.

STANLEY *slowly sits at the table, left.*

Do you know them?

STANLEY *does not answer.*

Stan, they won't wake you up, I promise. I'll tell them they must be quiet.

STANLEY *sits still.*

They won't be here long, Stan. I'll still bring you up your early morning tea.

STANLEY *sits still.*

You mustn't be sad today. It's your birthday.

A pause.

STANLEY (*dumbly*). Uh?

MEG. It's your birthday, Stan. I was going to keep it a secret until tonight.

STANLEY. No.

MEG. It is. I've brought you a present. (*She goes to the sideboard, picks up the parcel, and places it on the table in front of him.*) Here. Go on. Open it.

STANLEY. What's this?

MEG. It's your present.

STANLEY. This isn't my birthday, Meg.

MEG. Of course it is. Open your present.

He stares at the parcel, slowly stands, and opens it. He takes out a boy's drum.

STANLEY (*flatly*). It's a drum. A boy's drum.

MEG (*tenderly*). It's because you haven't got a piano. (*He stares at her, then turns and walks towards the door, left.*) Aren't you going to give me a kiss? (*He turns sharply, and stops. He walks back towards her slowly. He stops at her chair, looking down upon her. Pause. His shoulders sag, he bends and kisses her on the cheek.*) There are some sticks in there. (STANLEY *looks into the parcel. He takes out two drumsticks. He taps them together. He looks at her.*)

STANLEY. Shall I put it round my neck?

She watches him, uncertainly. He hangs the drum around his neck, taps it gently with the sticks, then marches round the table, beating it regularly. MEG, *pleased, watches him. Still beating it regularly, he begins to go round the table a second time. Halfway round the beat becomes erratic, uncontrolled.* MEG *expresses dismay. He arrives at her chair, banging the drum, his face and the drumbeat now savage and possessed.*

Curtain

Act Two

MCCANN *is sitting at the table tearing a sheet of newspaper into five equal strips. It is evening. After a few moments* STANLEY *enters from the left. He stops upon seeing* MCCANN, *and watches him. He then walks towards the kitchen, stops, and speaks.*

STANLEY. Evening.
MCCANN. Evening.

> *Chuckles are heard from outside the back door, which is open.*

STANLEY. Very warm tonight. (*He turns towards the back door, and back.*) Someone out there?

> MCCANN *tears another length of paper.* STANLEY *goes into the kitchen and pours a glass of water. He drinks it looking through the hatch. He puts the glass down, comes out of the kitchen and walks quickly towards the door, left.* MCCANN *rises and intercepts him.*

MCCANN. I don't think we've met.
STANLEY. No, we haven't.
MCCANN. My name's McCann.
STANLEY. Staying here long?
MCCANN. Not long. What's your name?
STANLEY. Webber.
MCCANN. I'm glad to meet you, sir. (*He offers his hand.* STANLEY *takes it, and* MCCANN *holds the grip.*) Many happy returns of the day. (STANLEY *withdraws his hand. They face each other.*) Were you going out?
STANLEY. Yes.
MCCANN. On your birthday?
STANLEY. Yes. Why not?

MCCANN. But they're holding a party here for you tonight.
STANLEY. Oh really? That's unfortunate.
MCCANN. Ah no. It's very nice.

Voices from outside the back door.

STANLEY. I'm sorry. I'm not in the mood for a party tonight.
MCCANN. Oh, is that so? I'm sorry.
STANLEY. Yes, I'm going out to celebrate quietly, on my own.
MCCANN. That's a shame.

They stand.

STANLEY. Well, if you'd move out of my way—
MCCANN. But everything's laid on. The guests are expected.
STANLEY. Guests? What guests?
MCCANN. Myself for one. I had the honour of an invitation.

MCCANN *begins to whistle "The Mountains of Morne".*

STANLEY (*moving away*). I wouldn't call it an honour, would
　you? It'll just be another booze-up.

MCCANN. But it is an honour.
STANLEY. I'd say you were exaggerating.
MCCANN. Oh no. I'd say it was an honour.
STANLEY. I'd say that was plain stupid.
MCCANN. Ah no.

They stare at each other.

STANLEY. Who are the other guests?
MCCANN. A young lady.
STANLEY. Oh yes? And. . . .?
MCCANN. My friend.
STANLEY. Your friend?

MCCANN. That's right. It's all laid on.

STANLEY *walks round the table towards the door.* MCCANN
meets him.

STANLEY. Excuse me.

MCCANN. Where are you going?

STANLEY. I want to go out.

MCCANN. Why don't you stay here?

STANLEY *moves away, to the right of the table.*

STANLEY. So you're down here on holiday?

MCCANN. A short one. (STANLEY *picks up a strip of paper.*
MCCANN *moves in.*) Mind that.

STANLEY. What is it?

MCCANN. Mind it. Leave it.

STANLEY. I've got a feeling we've met before.

MCCANN. No we haven't.

STANLEY. Ever been anywhere near Maidenhead?

MCCANN. No.

STANLEY. There's a Fuller's teashop. I used to have my tea
there.

MCCANN. I don't know it.

STANLEY. And a Boots Library. I seem to connect you with
the High Street.

MCCANN. Yes?

STANLEY. A charming town, don't you think?

MCCANN. I don't know it.

STANLEY. Oh no. A quiet, thriving community. I was born
and brought up there. I lived well away from the main road.

MCCANN. Yes?

Pause.

STANLEY. You're here on a short stay?

MCCANN. That's right.

STANLEY. You'll find it very bracing.

MCCANN. Do you find it bracing?

STANLEY. Me? No. But you will. (*He sits at the table.*) I like
it here, but I'll be moving soon. Back home. I'll stay there
too, this time. No place like home. (*He laughs.*) I wouldn't
have left, but business calls. Business called, and I had to
leave for a bit. You know how it is.

MCCANN (*sitting at the table, left*). You in business?

STANLEY. No. I think I'll give it up. I've got a small private
income, you see. I think I'll give it up. Don't like being
away from home. I used to live very quietly—played records,
that's about all. Everything delivered to the door. Then I
started a little private business, in a small way, and it com-
pelled me to come down here—kept me longer than I
expected. You never get used to living in someone else's
house. Don't you agree? I lived so quietly. You can only
appreciate what you've had when things change. That's what
they say, isn't it? Cigarette?

MCCANN. I don't smoke.

STANLEY *lights a cigarette. Voices from the back.*

STANLEY. Who's out there?

MCCANN. My friend and the man of the house.

STANLEY. You know what? To look at me, I bet you wouldn't
think I'd led such a quiet life. The lines on my face, eh? It's
the drink. Been drinking a bit down here. But what I mean
is . . . you know how it is . . . away from your own . . .
all wrong, of course . . . I'll be all right when I get back
. . . but what I mean is, the way some people look at me
you'd think I was a different person. I suppose I have
changed, but I'm still the same man that I always was. I
mean, you wouldn't think, to look at me, really . . . I mean,
not really, that I was the sort of bloke to—to cause any
trouble, would you? (MCCANN *looks at him.*) Do you know
what I mean?

MCCANN. No. (*As* STANLEY *picks up a strip of paper.*) Mind
that.

STANLEY (*quickly*). Why are you down here?

MCCANN. A short holiday.

STANLEY. This is a ridiculous house to pick on. (*He rises.*)

MCCANN. Why?

STANLEY. Because it's not a boarding house. It never was.

MCCANN. Sure it is.

STANLEY. Why did you choose this house?

MCCANN. You know, sir, you're a bit depressed for a man on his birthday.

STANLEY (*sharply*). Why do you call me sir?

MCCANN. You don't like it?

STANLEY (*to the table.*) Listen. Don't call me sir.

MCCANN. I won't, if you don't like it.

STANLEY (*moving away*). No. Anyway, this isn't my birthday.

MCCANN. No?

STANLEY. No. It's not till next month.

MCCANN. Not according to the lady.

STANLEY. Her? She's crazy. Round the bend.

MCCANN. That's a terrible thing to say.

STANLEY (*to the table*). Haven't you found that out yet? There's a lot you don't know. I think someone's leading you up the garden path.

MCCANN. Who would do that?

STANLEY (*leaning across the table*). That woman is mad!

MCCANN. That's slander.

STANLEY. And you don't know what you're doing.

MCCANN. Your cigarette is near that paper.

> *Voices from the back.*

STANLEY. Where the hell are they? (*Stubbing his cigarette.*) Why don't they come in? What are they doing out there?

MCCANN. You want to steady yourself.

> STANLEY *crosses to him and grips his arm.*

STANLEY (*urgently*). Look—

MCCANN. Don't touch me.

STANLEY. Look. Listen a minute.

MCCANN. Let go my arm.

STANLEY. Look. Sit down a minute.

MCCANN (*savagely, hitting his arm*). Don't do that!

> STANLEY *backs across the stage, holding his arm.*

STANLEY. Listen. You knew what I was talking about before, didn't you?

MCCANN. I don't know what you're at at all.

STANLEY. It's a mistake! Do you understand?

MCCANN. You're in a bad state, man.

STANLEY (*whispering, advancing*). Has he told you anything? Do you know what you're here for? Tell me. You needn't be frightened of me. Or hasn't he told you?

MCCANN. Told me what?

STANLEY (*hissing*). I've explained to you, damn you, that all those years I lived in Basingstoke I never stepped outside the door.

MCCANN. You know, I'm flabbergasted with you.

STANLEY (*reasonably*). Look. You look an honest man. You're being made a fool of, that's all. You understand? Where do you come from?

MCCANN. Where do you think?

STANLEY. I know Ireland very well. I've many friends there. I love that country and I admire and trust its people. I trust them. They respect the truth and they have a sense of humour. I think their policemen are wonderful. I've been there. I've never seen such sunsets. What about coming out to have a drink with me? There's a pub down the road serves draught Guinness. Very difficult to get in these parts —(*He breaks off. The voices draw nearer.* GOLDBERG *and* PETEY *enter from the back door.*)

GOLDBERG (*as he enters*). A mother in a million. (*He sees* STANLEY.) Ah.

PETEY. Oh hullo, Stan. You haven't met Stanley, have you, Mr Goldberg?

GOLDBERG. I haven't had the pleasure.

PETEY. Oh well, this is Mr Goldberg, this is Mr Webber.

GOLDBERG. Pleased to meet you.

PETEY. We were just getting a bit of air in the garden.

GOLDBERG. I was telling Mr Boles about my old mum. What days. (*He sits at the table, right.*) Yes. When I was a youngster, of a Friday, I used to go for a walk down the canal with a girl who lived down my road. A beautiful girl. What a voice that bird had! A nightingale, my word of honour. Good? Pure? She wasn't a Sunday school teacher for nothing. Anyway, I'd leave her with a little kiss on the cheek —I never took liberties—we weren't like the young men these days in those days. We knew the meaning of respect. So I'd give her a peck and I'd bowl back home. Humming away I'd be, past the children's playground. I'd tip my hat to the toddlers, I'd give a helping hand to a couple of stray dogs, everything came natural. I can see it like yesterday. The sun falling behind the dog stadium. Ah! (*He leans back contentedly.*)

MCCANN. Like behind the town hall.

GOLDBERG. What town hall?

MCCANN. In Carrikmacross.

GOLDBERG. There's no comparison. Up the street, into my gate, inside the door, home. "Simey!" my old mum used to shout, "quick before it gets cold." And there on the table what would I see? The nicest piece of gefilte fish you could wish to find on a plate.

MCCANN. I thought your name was Nat.

GOLDBERG. She called me Simey.

PETEY. Yes, we all remember our childhood.

GOLDBERG. Too true. Eh, Mr Webber, what do you say? Childhood. Hot water bottles. Hot milk. Pancakes. Soap suds. What a life.

Pause.

PETEY (*rising from the table*). Well, I'll have to be off.

GOLDBERG. Off?

PETEY. It's my chess night.

GOLDBERG. You're not staying for the party?

PETEY. No, I'm sorry, Stan. I didn't know about it till just now. And we've got a game on. I'll try and get back early.

GOLDBERG. We'll save some drink for you, all right? Oh, that reminds me. You'd better go and collect the bottles.

MCCANN. Now?

GOLDBERG. Of course, now. Time's getting on. Round the corner, remember? Mention my name.

PETEY. I'm coming your way.

GOLDBERG. Beat him quick and come back, Mr Boles.

PETEY. Do my best. See you later, Stan.

> PETEY *and* MCCANN *go out, left.* STANLEY *moves to the centre.*

GOLDBERG. A warm night.

STANLEY (*turning*). Don't mess me about!

GOLDBERG. I beg your pardon?

STANLEY (*moving downstage*). I'm afraid there's been a mistake. We're booked out. Your room is taken. Mrs Boles forgot to tell you. You'll have to find somewhere else.

GOLDBERG. Are you the manager here?

STANLEY. That's right.

GOLDBERG. Is it a good game?

STANLEY. I run the house. I'm afraid you and your friend will have to find other accommodation.

GOLDBERG (*rising*). Oh, I forgot, I must congratulate you on your birthday. (*Offering his hand.*) Congratulations.

STANLEY (*ignoring hand*). Perhaps you're deaf.

GOLDBERG. No, what makes you think that? As a matter of fact, every single one of my senses is at its peak. Not bad going, eh? For a man past fifty. But a birthday, I always feel, is a great occasion, taken too much for granted these days. What a thing to celebrate—birth! Like getting up in the morning. Marvellous! Some people don't like the idea of getting up in the morning. I've heard them. Getting up in the morning, they say, what is it? Your skin's crabby, you need a shave, your eyes are full of muck, your mouth is like a boghouse, the palms of your hands are full of sweat, your nose is clogged up, your feet stink, what are you but a corpse waiting to be washed? Whenever I hear that point of view I feel cheerful. Because I know what it is to wake up with the sun shining, to the sound of the lawnmower, all the little birds, the smell of the grass, church bells, tomato juice—

STANLEY. Get out.

Enter MCCANN, *with bottles.*

Get that drink out. These are unlicensed premises.

GOLDBERG. You're in a terrible humour today, Mr Webber. And on your birthday too, with the good lady getting her strength up to give you a party.

MCCANN *puts the bottles on the sideboard.*

STANLEY. I told you to get those bottles out.

GOLDBERG. Mr Webber, sit down a minute.

STANLEY. Let me—just make this clear. You don't bother me. To me, you're nothing but a dirty joke. But I have a responsibility towards the people in this house. They've been down here too long. They've lost their sense of smell. I haven't. And nobody's going to take advantage of them while I'm here. (*A little less forceful.*) Anyway, this house isn't your cup of tea. There's nothing here for you, from any angle, any angle. So why don't you just go, without any more fuss?

GOLDBERG. Mr Webber, sit down.

STANLEY. It's no good starting any kind of trouble.

GOLDBERG. Sit down.

STANLEY. Why should I?

GOLDBERG. If you want to know the truth, Webber, you're beginning to get on my breasts.

STANLEY. Really? Well, that's—

GOLDBERG. Sit down.

STANLEY. No.

GOLDBERG *sighs, and sits at the table right.*

GOLDBERG. McCann.

MCCANN. Nat?

GOLDBERG. Ask him to sit down.

MCCANN. Yes, Nat. (MCCANN *moves to* STANLEY.) Do you mind sitting down?

STANLEY. Yes, I do mind.

MCCANN. Yes now, but—it'd be better if you did.

STANLEY. Why don't you sit down?

MCCANN. No, not me—you.

STANLEY. No thanks.

Pause.

MCCANN. Nat.

GOLDBERG. What?

MCCANN. He won't sit down.

GOLDBERG. Well, ask him.

MCCANN. I've asked him.

GOLDBERG. Ask him again.

MCCANN (*to* STANLEY). Sit down.

STANLEY. Why?

MCCANN. You'd be more comfortable.

STANLEY. So would you.

Pause.

MCCANN. All right. If you will I will.

STANLEY. You first.

MCCANN *slowly sits at the table, left*

MCCANN. Well?

STANLEY. Right. Now you've both had a rest you can get out!

MCCANN (*rising*). That's a dirty trick! I'll kick the shite out of him!

GOLDBERG (*rising*). No! I have stood up.

MCCANN. Sit down again!

GOLDBERG. Once I'm up I'm up.

STANLEY. Same here.

MCCANN (*moving to* STANLEY). You've made Mr Goldberg stand up.

STANLEY (*his voice rising*). It'll do him good!

MCCANN. Get in that seat.

GOLDBERG. McCann.

MCCANN. Get down in that seat!

GOLDBERG (*crossing to him*). Webber. (*Quietly.*) SIT DOWN. (*Silence.* STANLEY *begins to whistle "The Mountains of Morne". He strolls casually to the chair at the table. They watch him. He stops whistling. Silence. He sits.*)

STANLEY. You'd better be careful.

GOLDBERG. Webber, what were you doing yesterday?

STANLEY. Yesterday?

GOLDBERG. And the day before. What did you do the day before that?

STANLEY. What do you mean?

GOLDBERG. Why are you wasting everybody's time, Webber? Why are you getting in everybody's way?

STANLEY. Me? What are you—

GOLDBERG. I'm telling you, Webber. You're a washout. Why are you getting on everybody's wick? Why are you driving that old lady off her conk?

MCCANN. He likes to do it!

GOLDBERG. Why do you behave so badly, Webber? Why do you force that old man out to play chess?

STANLEY. Me?

GOLDBERG. Why do you treat that young lady like a leper?

She's not the leper, Webber!

STANLEY. What the—

GOLDBERG. What did you wear last week, Webber? Where do
you keep your suits?

MCCANN. Why did you leave the organization?

GOLDBERG. What would your old mum say, Webber?

MCCANN. Why did you betray us?

GOLDBERG. You hurt me, Webber. You're playing a dirty
game.

MCCANN. That's a Black and Tan fact.

GOLDBERG. Who does he think he is?

MCCANN. Who do you think you are?

STANLEY. You're on the wrong horse.

GOLDBERG. When did you come to this place?

STANLEY. Last year.

GOLDBERG. Where did you come from?

STANLEY. Somewhere else.

GOLDBERG. Why did you come here?

STANLEY. My feet hurt!

GOLDBERG. Why did you stay?

STANLEY. I had a headache!

GOLDBERG. Did you take anything for it?

STANLEY. Yes.

GOLDBERG. What?

STANLEY. Fruit salts!

GOLDBERG. Enos or Andrews?

STANLEY. En— An—

GOLDBERG. Did you stir properly? Did they fizz?

STANLEY. Now, now, wait, you—

GOLDBERG. Did they fizz? Did they fizz or didn't they fizz?

MCCANN. He doesn't know!

GOLDBERG. You don't know. When did you last have a bath?

STANLEY. I have one every—

GOLDBERG. Don't lie.

MCCANN. You betrayed the organization. I know him!

STANLEY. You don't!

GOLDBERG. What can you see without your glasses?

STANLEY. Anything.

GOLDBERG. Take off his glasses.

> MCCANN *snatches his glasses and as* STANLEY *rises, reaching for them, takes his chair downstage centre, below the table,* STANLEY *stumbling as he follows.* STANLEY *clutches the chair and stays bent over it.*

Webber, you're a fake. (*They stand on each side of the chair.*) When did you last wash up a cup?

STANLEY. The Christmas before last.

GOLDBERG. Where?

STANLEY. Lyons Corner House.

GOLDBERG. Which one?

STANLEY. Marble Arch.

GOLDBERG. Where was your wife?

STANLEY. In—

GOLDBERG. Answer.

STANLEY (*turning, crouched*). What wife?

GOLDBERG. What have you done with your wife?

MCCANN. He's killed his wife!

GOLDBERG. Why did you kill your wife?

STANLEY (*sitting, his back to the audience*). What wife?

MCCANN. How did he kill her?

GOLDBERG. How did you kill her?

MCCANN. You throttled her.

GOLDBERG. With arsenic.

MCCANN. There's your man!

GOLDBERG. Where's your old mum?

STANLEY. In the sanatorium.

MCCANN. Yes!

GOLDBERG. Why did you never get married?

MCCANN. She was waiting at the porch.

GOLDBERG. You skeddadled from the wedding.

MCCANN. He left her in the lurch.

GOLDBERG. You left her in the pudding club.

MCCANN. She was waiting at the church.

GOLDBERG. Webber! Why did you change your name?

STANLEY. I forgot the other one.

GOLDBERG. What's your name now?

STANLEY. Joe Soap.

GOLDBERG. You stink of sin.

MCCANN. I can smell it.

GOLDBERG. Do you recognise an external force?

STANLEY. What?

GOLDBERG. Do you recognise an external force?

MCCANN. That's the question!

GOLDBERG. Do you recognise an external force, responsible for you, suffering for you?

STANLEY. It's late.

GOLDBERG. Late! Late enough! When did you last pray?

MCCANN. He's sweating!

GOLDBERG. When did you last pray?

MCCANN. He's sweating!

GOLDBERG. Is the number 846 possible or necessary?

STANLEY. Neither.

GOLDBERG. Wrong! Is the number 846 possible or necessary?

STANLEY. Both.

GOLDBERG. Wrong! It's necessary but not possible.

STANLEY. Both.

GOLDBERG. Wrong! Why do you think the number 846 is necessarily possible?

STANLEY. Must be.

GOLDBERG. Wrong! It's only necessarily necessary! We admit possibility only after we grant necessity. It is possible because necessary but by no means necessary through possibility. The possibility can only be assumed after the proof of necessity.

MCCANN. Right!

GOLDBERG. Right? Of course right! We're right and you're
wrong, Webber, all along the line.

MCCANN. All along the line!

GOLDBERG. Where is your lechery leading you?

MCCANN. You'll pay for this.

GOLDBERG. You stuff yourself with dry toast.

MCCANN. You contaminate womankind.

GOLDBERG. Why don't you pay the rent?

MCCANN. Mother defiler!

GOLDBERG. Why do you pick your nose?

MCCANN. I demand justice!

GOLDBERG. What's your trade?

MCCANN. What about Ireland?

GOLDBERG. What's your trade?

STANLEY. I play the piano.

GOLDBERG. How many fingers do you use?

STANLEY. No hands!

GOLDBERG. No society would touch you. Not even a building
society.

MCCANN. You're a traitor to the cloth.

GOLDBERG. What do you use for pyjamas?

STANLEY. Nothing.

GOLDBERG. You verminate the sheet of your birth.

MCCANN. What about the Albigensenist heresy?

GOLDBERG. Who watered the wicket in Melbourne?

MCCANN. What about the blessed Oliver Plunkett?

GOLDBERG. Speak up, Webber. Why did the chicken cross the
road?

STANLEY. He wanted to—he wanted to—he wanted to. . . .

MCCANN. He doesn't know!

GOLDBERG. Why did the chicken cross the road?

STANLEY. He wanted to—he wanted to. . . .

GOLDBERG. Why did the chicken cross the road?

STANLEY. He wanted. . . .

MCCANN. He doesn't know. He doesn't know which came first!

GOLDBERG. Which came first?

MCCANN. Chicken? Egg? Which came first?

GOLDBERG and MCCANN. Which came first? Which came
first? Which came first?

> STANLEY *screams.*

GOLDBERG. He doesn't know. Do you know your own face?

MCCANN. Wake him up. Stick a needle in his eye.

GOLDBERG. You're a plague, Webber. You're an overthrow.

MCCANN. You're what's left!

GOLDBERG. But we've got the answer to you. We can sterilise
you.

MCCANN. What about Drogheda?

GOLDBERG. Your bite is dead. Only your pong is left.

MCCANN. You betrayed our land.

GOLDBERG. You betray our breed.

MCCANN. Who are you, Webber?

GOLDBERG. What makes you think you exist?

MCCANN. You're dead.

GOLDBERG. You're dead. You can't live, you can't think, you
can't love. You're dead. You're a plague gone bad. There's
no juice in you. You're nothing but an odour!

> *Silence. They stand over him. He is crouched in the chair.
> He looks up slowly and kicks* GOLDBERG *in the stomach.*
> GOLDBERG *falls.* STANLEY *stands.* MCCANN *seizes a chair
> and lifts it above his head.* STANLEY *seizes a chair and
> covers his head with it.* MCCANN *and* STANLEY *circle.*

GOLDBERG. Steady, McCann.

STANLEY (*circling*). Uuuuuhhhhh!

MCCANN. Right, Judas.

GOLDBERG (*rising*). Steady, McCann.

MCCANN. Come on!

STANLEY. Uuuuuuuhhhhh!

MCCANN. He's sweating.

STANLEY. Uuuuuhhhhh!

GOLDBERG. Easy, McCann.

MCCANN. The bastard sweatpig is sweating.

> *A loud drumbeat off left, descending the stairs.* GOLDBERG
> *takes the chair from* STANLEY. *They put the chairs down.*
> *They stop still. Enter* MEG, *in evening dress, holding sticks*
> *and drum.*

MEG. I brought the drum down. I'm dressed for the party.

GOLDBERG. Wonderful.

MEG. You like my dress?

GOLDBERG. Wonderful. Out of this world.

MEG. I know. My father gave it to me. (*Placing drum on table.*)
Doesn't it make a beautiful noise?

GOLDBERG. It's a fine piece of work. Maybe Stan'll play us a
little tune afterwards.

MEG. Oh yes. Will you, Stan?

STANLEY. Could I have my glasses?

GOLDBERG. Ah yes. (*He holds his hand out to* MCCANN.
MCCANN *passes him his glasses.*) Here they are. (*He holds
them out for* STANLEY, *who reaches for them.*) Here they are.
(STANLEY *takes them.*) Now. What have we got here?
Enough to scuttle a liner. We've got four bottles of Scotch
and one bottle of Irish.

MEG. Oh, Mr Goldberg, what should I drink?

GOLDBERG. Glasses, glasses first. Open the Scotch, McCann.

MEG (*at the sideboard*). Here's my very best glasses in here.

MCCANN. I don't drink Scotch.

GOLDBERG. You've got the Irish.

MEG (*bringing the glasses*). Here they are.

GOLDBERG. Good. Mrs Boles, I think Stanley should pour
the toast, don't you?

MEG. Oh yes. Come on, Stanley. (STANLEY *walks slowly to the*
table.) Do you like my dress, Mr Goldberg?

GOLDBERG. It's out on its own. Turn yourself round a minute.
I used to be in the business. Go on, walk up there.

MEG. Oh no.

GOLDBERG. Don't be shy. (*He slaps her bottom.*)

MEG. Oooh!

GOLDBERG. Walk up the boulevard. Let's have a look at you. What a carriage. What's your opinion, McCann? Like a Countess, nothing less. Madam, now turn about and promenade to the kitchen. What a deportment!

MCCANN (*to* STANLEY). You can pour my Irish too.

GOLDBERG. You look like a Gladiola.

MEG. Stan, what about my dress?

GOLDBERG. One for the lady, one for the lady. Now madam—your glass.

MEG. Thank you.

GOLDBERG. Lift your glasses, ladies and gentlemen. We'll drink a toast.

MEG. Lulu isn't here.

GOLDBERG. It's past the hour. Now—who's going to propose the toast? Mrs Boles, it can only be you.

MEG. Me?

GOLDBERG. Who else?

MEG. But what do I say?

GOLDBERG. Say what you feel. What you honestly feel. (MEG *looks uncertain.*) It's Stanley's birthday. Your Stanley. Look at him. Look at him and it'll come. Wait a minute, the light's too strong. Let's have proper lighting. McCann, have you got your torch?

MCCANN (*bringing a small torch from his pocket*). Here.

GOLDBERG. Switch out the light and put on your torch. (MCCANN *goes to the door, switches off the light, comes back, shines the torch on* MEG. *Outside the window there is still a faint light.*) Not on the lady, on the gentleman! You must shine it on the birthday boy. (MCCANN *shines the torch in* STANLEY'S *face.*) Now, Mrs Boles, it's all yours.

Pause.

MEG. I don't know what to say.

GOLDBERG. Look at him. Just look at him.

MEG. Isn't the light in his eyes?

GOLDBERG. No, no. Go on.

MEG. Well—it's very, very nice to be here tonight, in my house, and I want to propose a toast to Stanley, because it's his birthday, and he's lived here for a long while now, and he's my Stanley now. And I think he's a good boy, although sometimes he's bad. (*An appreciative laugh from* GOLDBERG.) And he's the only Stanley I know, and I know him better than all the world, although he doesn't think so. ("*Hear—hear*" *from* GOLDBERG.) Well, I could cry because I'm so happy, having him here and not gone away, on his birthday, and there isn't anything I wouldn't do for him, and all you good people here tonight. . . . (*She sobs.*)

GOLDBERG. Beautiful! A beautiful speech. Put the light on, McCann. (MCCANN *goes to the door.* STANLEY *remains still.*) That was a lovely toast. (*The light goes on.* LULU *enters from the door, left.* GOLDBERG *comforts* MEG.) Buck up now. Come on, smile at the birdy. That's better. Ah, look who's here.

MEG. Lulu.

GOLDBERG. How do you do, Lulu? I'm Nat Goldberg.

LULU. Hallo.

GOLDBERG. Stanley, a drink for your guest. You just missed the toast, my dear, and what a toast.

LULU. Did I?

GOLDBERG. Stanley, a drink for your guest. Stanley. (STANLEY *hands a glass to* LULU.) Right. Now raise your glasses. Everyone standing up? No, not you, Stanley. You must sit down.

MCCANN. Yes, that's right. He must sit down.

GOLDBERG. You don't mind sitting down a minute? We're going to drink to you.

MEG. Come on!

LULU. Come on!

STANLEY *sits in a chair at the table.*

GOLDBERG. Right. Now Stanley's sat down. (*Taking the stage.*) Well, I want to say first that I've never been so touched to the heart as by the toast we've just heard. How often, in this day and age, do you come across real, true warmth? Once in a lifetime. Until a few minutes ago, ladies and gentlemen, I, like all of you, was asking the same question. What's happened to the love, the bonhomie, the unashamed expression of affection of the day before yesterday, that our mums taught us in the nursery?

MCCANN. Gone with the wind.

GOLDBERG. That's what I thought, until today. I believe in a good laugh, a day's fishing, a bit of gardening. I was very proud of my old greenhouse, made out of my own spit and faith. That's the sort of man I am. Not size but quality. A little Austin, tea in Fullers, a library book from Boots, and I'm satisfied. But just now, I say just now, the lady of the house said her piece and I for one am knocked over by the sentiments she expressed. Lucky is the man who's at the receiving end, that's what I say. (*Pause.*) How can I put it to you? We all wander on our tod through this world. It's a lonely pillow to kip on. Right!

LULU (*admiringly*). Right!

GOLDBERG. Agreed. But tonight, Lulu, McCann, we've known a great fortune. We've heard a lady extend the sum total of her devotion, in all its pride, plume and peacock, to a member of her own living race. Stanley, my heartfelt congratulations. I wish you, on behalf of us all, a happy birthday. I'm sure you've never been a prouder man than you are today. Mazoltov! And may we only meet at Simchahs! (*LULU and MEG applaud.*) Turn out the light, McCann, while we drink the toast.

LULU. That was a wonderful speech.

MCCANN *switches out the light, comes back, and shines the torch in* STANLEY'S *face. The light outside the window is fainter.*

GOLDBERG. Lift your glasses. Stanley—happy birthday.

MCCANN. Happy birthday.

LULU. Happy birthday.

MEG. Many happy returns of the day, Stan.

GOLDBERG. And well over the fast.

They all drink.

MEG (*kissing him*). Oh, Stanny. . . .

GOLDBERG. Lights!

MCCANN. Right! (*He switches on the lights.*)

MEG. Clink my glass, Stan.

LULU. Mr Goldberg—

GOLDBERG. Call me Nat.

MEG (*to* MCCANN). You clink my glass.

LULU (*to* GOLDBERG). You're empty. Let me fill you up.

GOLDBERG. It's a pleasure.

LULU. You're a marvellous speaker, Nat, you know that? Where did you learn to speak like that?

GOLDBERG. You liked it, eh?

LULU. Oh yes!

GOLDBERG. Well, my first chance to stand up and give a lecture was at the Ethical Hall, Bayswater. A wonderful opportunity. I'll never forget it. They were all there that night. Charlotte Street was empty. Of course, that's a good while ago.

LULU. What did you speak about?

GOLDBERG. The Necessary and the Possible. It went like a bomb. Since then I always speak at weddings.

STANLEY *is still.* GOLDBERG *sits left of the table.* MEG *joins* MCCANN *downstage, right,* LULU *is downstage, left.* MCCANN *pours more Irish from the bottle, which he carries, into his glass.*

MEG. Let's have some of yours.

MCCANN. In that?

MEG. Yes.

MCCANN. Are you used to mixing them?

MEG. No.

MCCANN. Give me your glass.

> MEG *sits on a shoe-box, downstage, right.* LULU, *at the table, pours more drink for* GOLDBERG *and herself, and gives* GOLDBERG *his glass.*

GOLDBERG. Thank you.

MEG (*to* MCCANN). Do you think I should?

GOLDBERG. Lulu, you're a big bouncy girl. Come and sit on my lap.

MCCANN. Why not?

LULU. Do you think I should?

GOLDBERG. Try it.

MEG (*sipping*). Very nice.

LULU. I'll bounce up to the ceiling.

MCCANN. I don't know how you can mix that stuff.

GOLDBERG. Take a chance.

MEG (*to* MCCANN). Sit down on this stool.

> LULU *sits on* GOLDBERG'S *lap.*

MCCANN. This?

GOLDBERG. Comfortable?

LULU. Yes thanks.

MCCANN (*sitting*). It's comfortable.

GOLDBERG. You know, there's a lot in your eyes.

LULU. And in yours, too.

GOLDBERG. Do you think so?

LULU (*giggling*). Go on!

MCCANN (*to* MEG). Where'd you get it?

MEG. My father gave it to me.

LULU. I didn't know I was going to meet you here tonight.

MCCANN (*to* MEG). Ever been to Carrikmacross?

MEG (*drinking*). I've been to King's Cross.

LULU. You came right out of the blue, you know that?

GOLDBERG (*as she moves*). Mind how you go. You're cracking
a rib.

MEG (*standing*). I want to dance! (LULU *and* GOLDBERG *look
into each other's eyes.* MCCANN *drinks.* MEG *crosses to*
STANLEY). Stanley. Dance. (STANLEY *sits still.* MEG *dances
round the room alone, then comes back to* MCCANN, *who fills
her glass. She sits.*)

LULU (*to* GOLDBERG). Shall I tell you something?

GOLDBERG. What?

LULU. I trust you.

GOLDBERG (*lifting his glass*). Gesundheit.

LULU. Have you got a wife?

GOLDBERG. I had a wife. What a wife. Listen to this. Friday,
of an afternoon, I'd take myself for a little constitutional,
down over the park. Eh, do me a favour, just sit on the table
a minute, will you? (LULU *sits on the table. He stretches and
continues.*) A little constitutional. I'd say hullo to the little
boys, the little girls—I never made distinctions—and then
back I'd go, back to my bungalow with the flat roof. "Simey,"
my wife used to shout, "quick, before it gets cold!" And
there on the table what would I see? The nicest piece of rollmop and pickled cucumber you could wish to find on a plate.

LULU. I thought your name was Nat.

GOLDBERG. She called me Simey.

LULU. I bet you were a good husband.

GOLDBERG. You should have seen her funeral.

LULU. Why?

GOLDBERG (*draws in his breath and wags head*). What a funeral.

MEG (*to* MCCANN). My father was going to take me to Ireland
once. But then he went away by himself.

LULU (*to* GOLDBERG). Do you think you knew me when I was
a little girl?

GOLDBERG. Were you a nice little girl?

LULU. I was.

MEG. I don't know if he went to Ireland.

GOLDBERG. Maybe I played piggy-back with you.

LULU. Maybe you did.

MEG. He didn't take me.

GOLDBERG. Or pop goes the weasel.

LULU. Is that a game?

GOLDBERG. Sure it's a game!

MCCANN. Why didn't he take you to Ireland?

LULU. You're tickling me!

GOLDBERG. You should worry.

LULU. I've always liked older men. They can soothe you.

They embrace.

MCCANN. I know a place. Roscrea. Mother Nolan's.

MEG. There was a night-light in my room, when I was a little girl.

MCCANN. One time I stayed there all night with the boys. Singing and drinking all night.

MEG. And my Nanny used to sit up with me, and sing songs to me.

MCCANN. And a plate of fry in the morning. Now where am I?

MEG. My little room was pink. I had a pink carpet and pink curtains, and I had musical boxes all over the room. And they played me to sleep. And my father was a very big doctor. That's why I never had any complaints. I was cared for, and I had little sisters and brothers in other rooms, all different colours.

MCCANN. Tullamore, where are you?

MEG (*to* MCCANN). Give us a drop more.

MCCANN (*filling her glass and singing*). Glorio, Glorio, to the bold Fenian men!

MEG. Oh, what a lovely voice.

GOLDBERG. Give us a song, McCann.

LULU. A love song!

MCCANN (*reciting*). The night that poor Paddy was stretched, the boys they all paid him a visit.

GOLDBERG. A love song!

MCCANN (*in a full voice, sings*)

> Oh, the Garden of Eden has vanished, they say,
> But I know the lie of it still.
> Just turn to the left at the foot of Ben Clay
> And stop when halfway to Coote Hill.
> It's there you will find it, I know sure enough,
> And it's whispering over to me:
> Come back, Paddy Reilly, to Bally-James-Duff,
> Come home, Paddy Reilly, to me!

LULU (*to* GOLDBERG). You're the dead image of the first man I ever loved.

GOLDBERG. It goes without saying.

MEG (*rising*). I want to play a game!

GOLDBERG. A game?

LULU. What game?

MEG. Any game.

LULU (*jumping up*). Yes, let's play a game.

GOLDBERG. What game?

MCCANN. Hide and seek.

LULU. Blind man's buff.

MEG. Yes!

GOLDBERG. You want to play blind man's buff?

LULU and MEG. Yes!

GOLDBERG. All right. Blind man's buff. Come on! Everyone up! (*Rising.*) McCann. Stanley—Stanley!

MEG. Stanley. Up.

GOLDBERG. What's the matter with him?

MEG (*bending over him*). Stanley, we're going to play a game. Oh, come on, don't be sulky, Stan.

LULU. Come on.

STANLEY *rises.* MCCANN *rises.*

GOLDBERG. Right! Now—who's going to be blind first?

LULU. Mrs Boles.

MEG. Not me.

GOLDBERG. Of course you.

MEG. Who, me?

LULU (*taking her scarf from her neck*). Here you are.

MCCANN. How do you play this game?

LULU (*tying her scarf round* MEG'S *eyes*). Haven't you ever played blind man's buff? Keep still, Mrs Boles. You mustn't be touched. But you can't move after she's blind. You must stay where you are after she's blind. And if she touches you then you become blind. Turn round. How many fingers am I holding up?

MEG. I can't see.

LULU. Right.

GOLDBERG. Right! Everyone move about. McCann. Stanley. Now stop. Now still. Off you go!

STANLEY *is downstage, right,* MEG *moves about the room.* GOLDBERG *fondles* LULU *at arm's length.* MEG *touches* MCCANN.

MEG. Caught you!

LULU. Take off your scarf.

MEG. What lovely hair!

LULU (*untying the scarf*). There.

MEG. It's you!

GOLDBERG. Put it on, McCann.

LULU (*tying it on* MCCANN). There. Turn round. How many fingers am I holding up?

MCCANN. I don't know.

GOLDBERG. Right! Everyone move about. Right. Stop! Still!

MCCANN *begins to move.*

MEG. Oh, this is lovely!

GOLDBERG. Quiet! Tch, tch, tch. Now—all move again. Stop! Still!

> MCCANN *moves about.* GOLDBERG *fondles* LULU *at arm's length.* MCCANN *draws near* STANLEY. *He stretches his arm and touches* STANLEY'S *glasses.*

MEG. It's Stanley!

GOLDBERG (*to* LULU). Enjoying the game?

MEG. It's your turn, Stan.

> MCCANN *takes off the scarf.*

MCCANN (*to* STANLEY). I'll take your glasses.

> MCCANN *takes* STANLEY'S *glasses.*

MEG. Give me the scarf.

GOLDBERG (*holding* LULU). Tie his scarf, Mrs. Boles.

MEG. That's what I'm doing. (*To* STANLEY.) Can you see my nose?

GOLDBERG. He can't. Ready? Right! Everyone move. Stop! And still!

> STANLEY *stands blindfold.* MCCANN *backs slowly across the stage to the left. He breaks* STANLEY'S *glasses, snapping the frames.* MEG *is downstage, left,* LULU *and* GOLDBERG *upstage centre, close together.* STANLEY *begins to move, very slowly, across the stage to the left.* MCCANN *picks up the drum and places it sideways in* STANLEY'S *path.* STANLEY *walks into the drum and falls over with his foot caught in it.*

MEG. Ooh!

GOLDBERG. Sssh!

> STANLEY *rises. He begins to move towards* MEG, *dragging the drum on his foot. He reaches her and stops. His hands*

move towards her and they reach her throat. He begins to
strangle her. MCCANN *and* GOLDBERG *rush forward and*
throw him off.

BLACKOUT

There is now no light at all through the window. The stage
is in darkness.

LULU. The lights!

GOLDBERG. What's happened?

LULU. The lights!

MCCANN. Wait a minute.

GOLDBERG. Where is he?

MCCANN. Let go of me!

GOLDBERG. Who's this?

LULU. Someone's touching me!

MCCANN. Where is he?

MEG. Why has the light gone out?

GOLDBERG. Where's your torch? (MCCANN *shines the torch in*
    GOLDBERG'S *face.*) Not on me! (MCCANN *shifts the torch.*
    It is knocked from his hand and falls. It goes out.)

MCCANN. My torch!

LULU. Oh God!

GOLDBERG. Where's your torch? Pick up your torch!

MCCANN. I can't find it.

LULU. Hold me. Hold me.

GOLDBERG. Get down on your knees. Help him find the torch.

LULU. I can't.

MCCANN. It's gone.

MEG. Why has the light gone out?

GOLDBERG. Everyone quiet! Help him find the torch.

Silence. Grunts from MCCANN *and* GOLDBERG *on their*
knees. Suddenly there is a sharp, sustained rat-a-tat with a
stick on the side of the drum from the back of the room.
Silence. Whimpers from LULU.

GOLDBERG. Over here. McCann!

MCCANN. Here.

GOLDBERG. Come to me, come to me. Easy. Over there.

GOLDBERG *and* MCCANN *move up left of the table.*
STANLEY *moves down right of the table.* LULU *suddenly*
perceives him moving towards her, screams and faints.
GOLDBERG *and* MCCANN *turn and stumble against each*
other.

GOLDBERG. What is it?

MCCANN. Who's that?

GOLDBERG. What is it?

In the darkness STANLEY *picks up* LULU *and places her on*
the table.

MEG. It's Lulu!

GOLDBERG *and* MCCANN *move downstage, right.*

GOLDBERG. Where is she?

MCCANN. She fell.

GOLDBERG. Where?

MCCANN. About here.

GOLDBERG. Help me pick her up.

MCCANN (*moving downstage, left*). I can't find her.

GOLDBERG. She must be somewhere.

MCCANN. She's not here.

GOLDBERG (*moving downstage, left*). She must be.

MCCANN. She's gone.

MCCANN *finds the torch on the floor, shines it on the table*
and STANLEY. LULU *is lying spread-eagled on the table,*
STANLEY *bent over her.* STANLEY, *as soon as the torchlight*
hits him, begins to giggle. GOLDBERG *and* MCCANN *move*
towards him. He backs, giggling, the torch on his face. They
follow him upstage, left. He backs against the hatch, giggling.
The torch draws closer. His giggle rises and grows as he

flattens himself against the wall. Their figures converge upon him.

Curtain

Act Three

The next morning. PETEY *enters, left, with a newspaper and sits at the table. He begins to read.* MEG'S *voice comes through the kitchen hatch.*

MEG. Is that you, Stan? (*Pause.*) Stanny?

PETEY. Yes?

MEG. Is that you?

PETEY. It's me.

MEG (*appearing at the hatch*). Oh, it's you. I've run out of cornflakes.

PETEY. Well, what else have you got?

MEG. Nothing.

PETEY. Nothing?

MEG. Just a minute. (*She leaves the hatch and enters by the kitchen door.*) You got your paper?

PETEY. Yes.

MEG. Is it good?

PETEY. Not bad.

MEG. The two gentlemen had the last of the fry this morning.

PETEY. Oh, did they?

MEG. There's some tea in the pot though. (*She pours tea for him.*) I'm going out shopping in a minute. Get you something nice. I've got a splitting headache.

PETEY (*reading*). You slept like a log last night.

MEG. Did I?

PETEY. Dead out.

MEG. I must have been tired. (*She looks about the room and sees the broken drum in the fireplace.*) Oh, look. (*She rises and picks it up.*) The drum's broken. (PETEY *looks up.*) Why is it broken?

PETEY. I don't know.

She hits it with her hand.

MEG. It still makes a noise.

PETEY. You can always get another one.

MEG (*sadly*). It was probably broken in the party. I don't remember it being broken though, in the party. (*She puts it down.*) What a shame.

PETEY. You can always get another one, Meg.

MEG. Well, at least he did have it on his birthday, didn't he? Like I wanted him to.

PETEY (*reading*). Yes.

MEG. Have you seen him down yet? (PETEY *does not answer.*) Petey.

PETEY. What?

MEG. Have you seen him down?

PETEY. Who?

MEG. Stanley.

PETEY. No.

MEG. Nor have I. That boy should be up. He's late for his breakfast.

PETEY. There isn't any breakfast.

MEG. Yes, but he doesn't know that. I'm going to call him.

PETEY (*quickly*). No, don't do that, Meg. Let him sleep.

MEG. But you say he stays in bed too much.

PETEY. Let him sleep . . . this morning. Leave him.

MEG. I've been up once, with his cup of tea. But Mr McCann opened the door. He said they were talking. He said he'd made him one. He must have been up early. I don't know what they were talking about. I was surprised. Because Stanley's usually fast asleep when I wake him. But he wasn't this morning. I heard him talking. (*Pause.*) Do you think they know each other? I think they're old friends. Stanley had a lot of friends. I know he did. (*Pause.*) I didn't give him his tea. He'd already had one. I came down again and went on with my work. Then, after a bit, they came down to breakfast. Stanley must have gone to sleep again.

Pause.

PETEY. When are you going to do your shopping, Meg?

MEG. Yes, I must. (*Collecting the bag.*) I've got a rotten head-ache. (*She goes to the back door, stops suddenly and turns.*) Did you see what's outside this morning?

PETEY. What?

MEG. That big car.

PETEY. Yes.

MEG. It wasn't there yesterday. Did you . . . did you have a look inside it?

PETEY. I had a peep.

MEG (*coming down tensely, and whispering*). Is there anything in it?

PETEY. In it?

MEG. Yes.

PETEY. What do you mean, in it?

MEG. Inside it.

PETEY. What sort of thing?

MEG. Well . . . I mean . . . is there . . . is there a wheelbarrow in it?

PETEY. A wheelbarrow?

MEG. Yes.

PETEY. I didn't see one.

MEG. You didn't? Are you sure?

PETEY. What would Mr Goldberg want with a wheelbarrow?

MEG. Mr Goldberg?

PETEY. It's his car.

MEG (*relieved*). His car? Oh, I didn't know it was his car.

PETEY. Of course it's his car.

MEG. Oh, I feel better.

PETEY. What are you on about?

MEG. Oh, I do feel better.

PETEY. You go and get a bit of air.

MEG. Yes, I will. I will. I'll go and get the shopping. (*She goes towards the back door. A door slams upstairs. She turns.*) It's Stanley! He's coming down—what am I going to do about his breakfast? (*She rushes into the kitchen.*) Petey, what shall I give him? (*She looks through the hatch.*) There's no corn-flakes. (*They both gaze at the door. Enter* GOLDBERG. *He halts at the door, as he meets their gaze, then smiles.*)

GOLDBERG. A reception committee!

MEG. Oh, I thought it was Stanley.

GOLDBERG. You find a resemblance?

MEG. Oh no. You look quite different.

GOLDBERG (*coming into the room*). Different build, of course.

MEG (*entering from the kitchen*). I thought he was coming down for his breakfast. He hasn't had his breakfast yet.

GOLDBERG. Your wife makes a very nice cup of tea, Mr Boles, you know that?

PETEY. Yes, she does sometimes. Sometimes she forgets.

MEG. Is he coming down?

GOLDBERG. Down? Of course he's coming down. On a lovely sunny day like this he shouldn't come down? He'll be up and about in next to no time. (*He sits at the table.*) And what a breakfast he's going to get.

MEG. Mr Goldberg.

GOLDBERG. Yes?

MEG. I didn't know that was your car outside.

GOLDBERG. You like it?

MEG. Are you going to go for a ride?

GOLDBERG (*to* PETEY). A smart car, eh?

PETEY. Nice shine on it all right.

GOLDBERG. What is old is good, take my tip. There's room there. Room in the front, and room in the back. (*He strokes the teapot.*) The pot's hot. More tea, Mr Boles?

PETEY. No thanks.

GOLDBERG (*pouring tea*). That car? That car's never let me

down.

MEG. Are you going to go for a ride?

GOLDBERG *does not answer, drinks his tea.*

MEG. Well, I'd better be off now. (*She moves to the back door, and turns.*) Petey, when Stanley comes down. . . .

PETEY. Yes?

MEG. Tell him I won't be long.

PETEY. I'll tell him.

MEG (*vaguely*). I won't be long. (*She exits.*)

GOLDBERG (*sipping his tea*). A good woman. A charming woman. My mother was the same. My wife was identical.

PETEY. How is he this morning?

GOLDBERG. Who?

PETEY. Stanley. Is he any better?

GOLDBERG (*a little uncertainly*). Oh . . . a little better, I think, a little better. Of course, I'm not really qualified to say, Mr Boles. I mean, I haven't got the . . . the qualifications. The best thing would be if someone with the proper . . . mnn . . . qualifications . . . was to have a look at him. Someone with a few letters after his name. It makes all the difference.

PETEY. Yes.

GOLDBERG. Anyway, Dermot's with him at the moment. He's . . . keeping him company.

PETEY. Dermot?

GOLDBERG. Yes.

PETEY. It's a terrible thing.

GOLDBERG (*sighs*). Yes. The birthday celebration was too much for him.

PETEY. What came over him?

GOLDBERG (*sharply*). What came over him? Breakdown, Mr Boles. Pure and simple. Nervous breakdown.

PETEY. But what brought it on so suddenly?

GOLDBERG (*rising, and moving upstage*). Well, Mr Boles, it can happen in all sorts of ways. A friend of mine was telling me about it only the other day. We'd both been concerned with another case—not entirely similar, of course, but . . . quite alike, quite alike. (*He pauses.*) Anyway, he was telling me, you see, this friend of mine, that sometimes it happens gradual—day by day it grows and grows and grows . . . day by day. And then other times it happens all at once. Poof! Like that! The nerves break. There's no guarantee how it's going to happen, but with certain people . . . it's a foregone conclusion.

PETEY. Really?

GOLDBERG. Yes. This friend of mine—he was telling me about it—only the other day. (*He stands uneasily for a moment, then brings out a cigarette case and takes a cigarette.*) Have an Abdullah.

PETEY. No, no, I don't take them.

GOLDBERG. Once in a while I treat myself to a cigarette. An Abdullah, perhaps, or a . . . (*He snaps his fingers.*)

PETEY. What a night. (GOLDBERG *lights his cigarette with a lighter.*) Came in the front door and all the lights were out. Put a shilling in the slot, came in here and the party was over.

GOLDBERG (*coming downstage*). You put a shilling in the slot?

PETEY. Yes.

GOLDBERG. And the lights came on.

PETEY. Yes, then I came in here.

GOLDBERG (*with a short laugh*). I could have sworn it was a fuse.

PETEY (*continuing*). There was dead silence. Couldn't hear a thing. So I went upstairs and your friend—Dermot—met me on the landing. And he told me.

GOLDBERG (*sharply*). Who?

PETEY. Your friend—Dermot.

GOLDBERG (*heavily*). Dermot. Yes. (*He sits.*)

PETEY. They get over it sometimes though, don't they? I mean, they can recover from it, can't they?

GOLDBERG. Recover? Yes, sometimes they recover, in one way or another.

PETEY. I mean, he might have recovered by now, mightn't he?

GOLDBERG. It's conceivable. Conceivable.

PETEY *rises and picks up the teapot and cup.*

PETEY. Well, if he's no better by lunchtime I'll go and get hold of a doctor.

GOLDBERG (*briskly*). It's all taken care of, Mr Boles. Don't worry yourself.

PETEY (*dubiously*). What do you mean? (*Enter* MCCANN *with two suitcases.*) All packed up?

PETEY *takes the teapot and cups into the kitchen.* MCCANN *crosses left and puts down the suitcases. He goes up to the window and looks out.*

GOLDBERG. Well? (MCCANN *does not answer.*) McCann. I asked you well.

MCCANN (*without turning*). Well what?

GOLDBERG. What's what? (MCCANN *does not answer.*)

MCCANN (*turning to look at* GOLDBERG, *grimly*). I'm not going up there again.

GOLDBERG. Why not?

MCCANN. I'm not going up there again.

GOLDBERG. What's going on now?

MCCANN (*moving down*). He's quiet now. He stopped all that . . . talking a while ago.

PETEY *appears at the kitchen hatch, unnoticed.*

GOLDBERG. When will he be ready?

MCCANN (*sullenly*). You can go up yourself next time.

GOLDBERG. What's the matter with you?

MCCANN (*quietly*). I gave him. . . .

GOLDBERG. What?

MCCANN. I gave him his glasses.

GOLDBERG. Wasn't he glad to get them back?

MCCANN. The frames are bust.

GOLDBERG. How did that happen?

MCCANN. He tried to fit the eyeholes into his eyes. I left him doing it.

PETEY (*at the kitchen door*). There's some Sellotape somewhere. We can stick them together.

GOLDBERG *and* MCCANN *turn to see him. Pause.*

GOLDBERG. Sellotape? No, no, that's all right, Mr Boles. It'll keep him quiet for the time being, keep his mind off other things.

PETEY (*moving downstage*). What about a doctor?

GOLDBERG. It's all taken care of.

MCCANN *moves over right to the shoe-box, and takes out a brush and brushes his shoes.*

PETEY (*moves to the table*). I think he needs one.

GOLDBERG. I agree with you. It's all taken care of. We'll give him a bit of time to settle down, and then I'll take him to Monty.

PETEY. You're going to take him to a doctor?

GOLDBERG (*staring at him*). Sure. Monty.

Pause. MCCANN *brushes his shoes.*

So Mrs Boles has gone out to get us something nice for lunch?

PETEY. That's right.

GOLDBERG. Unfortunately we may be gone by then.

PETEY. Will you?

GOLDBERG. By then we may be gone.

Pause.

PETEY. Well, I think I'll see how my peas are getting on, in the meantime.

GOLDBERG. The meantime?

PETEY. While we're waiting.

GOLDBERG. Waiting for what? (PETEY *walks towards the back door*.) Aren't you going back to the beach?

PETEY. No, not yet. Give me a call when he comes down, will you, Mr Goldberg?

GOLDBERG (*earnestly*). You'll have a crowded beach today . . . on a day like this. They'll be lying on their backs, swimming out to sea. My life. What about the deck-chairs? Are the deck-chairs ready?

PETEY. I put them all out this morning.

GOLDBERG. But what about the tickets? Who's going to take the tickets?

PETEY. That's all right. That'll be all right. Mr Goldberg. Don't you worry about that. I'll be back.

He exits. GOLDBERG *rises, goes to the window and looks after him.* MCCANN *crosses to the table, left, sits, picks up the paper and begins to tear it into strips.*

GOLDBERG. Is everything ready?

MCCANN. Sure.

GOLDBERG *walks heavily, brooding, to the table. He sits right of it noticing what* MCCANN *is doing.*

GOLDBERG. Stop doing that!

MCCANN. What?

GOLDBERG. Why do you do that all the time? It's childish, it's pointless. It's without a solitary point.

MCCANN. What's the matter with you today?

GOLDBERG. Questions, questions. Stop asking me so many questions. What do you think I am?

MCCANN *studies him. He then folds the paper, leaving the strips inside.*

MCCANN. Well?

Pause. GOLDBERG *leans back in the chair, his eyes closed.*

MCCANN. Well?

GOLDBERG (*with fatigue*). Well what?

MCCANN. Do we wait or do we go and get him?

GOLDBERG (*slowly*). You want to go and get him?

MCCANN. I want to get it over.

GOLDBERG. That's understandable.

MCCANN. So do we wait or do we go and get him?

GOLDBERG (*interrupting*). I don't know why, but I feel knocked out. I feel a bit . . . It's uncommon for me.

MCCANN. Is that so?

GOLDBERG. It's unusual.

MCCANN (*rising swiftly and going behind* GOLDBERG'S *chair. Hissing*). Let's finish and go. Let's get it over and go. Get the thing done. Let's finish the bloody thing. Let's get the thing done and go!

> *Pause.*

Will I go up?

> *Pause.*

Nat!

> GOLDBERG *sits humped.* MCCANN *slips to his side.*

Simey!

GOLDBERG (*opening his eyes, regarding* MCCANN). What—did —you—call—me?

MCCANN. Who?

GOLDBERG (*murderously*). Don't call me that! (*He seizes* MCCANN *by the throat.*) NEVER CALL ME THAT!

MCCANN (*writhing*). Nat, Nat, Nat, NAT! I called you Nat. I was asking you, Nat. Honest to God. Just a question, that's all, just a question, do you see, do you follow me?

GOLDBERG (*jerking him away*). What question?

MCCANN. Will I go up?

GOLDBERG (*violently*). Up? I thought you weren't going to go up there again?

MCCANN. What do you mean? Why not?

GOLDBERG. You said so!

MCCANN. I never said that!

GOLDBERG. No?

MCCANN (*from the floor, to the room at large*). Who said that? I never said that! I'll go up now!

> *He jumps up and rushes to the door, left.*

GOLDBERG. Wait!

> *He stretches his arms to the arms of the chair.*

Come here.

> MCCANN *approaches him very slowly.*

I want your opinion. Have a look in my mouth.

> *He opens his mouth wide.*

Take a good look.

> MCCANN *looks.*

You know what I mean?

> MCCANN *peers.*

You know what? I've never lost a tooth. Not since the day I was born. Nothing's changed. (*He gets up.*) That's why I've reached my position, McCann. Because I've always been as fit as a fiddle. All my life I've said the same. Play up, play up, and play the game. Honour thy father and thy mother. All along the line. Follow the line, the line, McCann, and you can't go wrong. What do you think, I'm a self-made man? No! I sat where I was told to sit. I kept my eye on the ball. School? Don't talk to me about school. Top in all subjects. And for why? Because I'm telling you, I'm telling you, follow my line? Follow my mental? Learn by heart. Never write down a thing. And don't go too near the water.

And you'll find—that what I say is true.
Because I believe that the world . . . (*Vacant*.). . . .
Because I believe that the world . . . (*Desperate*.). . . .
BECAUSE I BELIEVE THAT THE WORLD . . . (*Lost*.). . . .

> *He sits in chair.*

Sit down, McCann, sit here where I can look at you.

> MCCANN *kneels in front of the table.*

(*Intensely, with growing certainty.*) My father said to me, Benny, Benny, he said, come here. He was dying. I knelt down. By him day and night. Who else was there? Forgive, Benny, he said, and let live. Yes, Dad. Go home to your wife. I will, Dad. Keep an eye open for low-lives, for schnorrers and for layabouts. He didn't mention names. I lost my life in the service of others, he said, I'm not ashamed. Do your duty and keep your observations. Always bid good morning to the neighbours. Never, never forget your family, for they are the rock, the constitution and the core! If you're ever in any difficulties Uncle Barney will see you in the clear. I knelt down. (*He kneels, facing* MCCANN.) I swore on the good book. And I knew the word I had to remember—Respect! Because McCann— (*Gently.*) Seamus—who came before your father? His father. And who came before him? Before him? . . . (*Vacant—triumphant.*) Who came before your father's father but your father's father's mother! Your great-gran-granny.

> *Silence. He slowly rises.*

And that's why I've reached my position, McCann. Because I've always been as fit as a fiddle. My motto. Work hard and play hard. Not a day's illness.

> GOLDBERG *sits.*

GOLDBERG. All the same, give me a blow. (*Pause.*) Blow in my mouth.

> MCCANN *stands, puts his hands on his knees, bends, and blows in* GOLDBERG'S *mouth.*

One for the road.

> MCCANN *blows again in his mouth.* GOLDBERG *breathes deeply, smiles.*

GOLDBERG. Right!

> *Enter* LULU. MCCANN *looks at them, and goes to the door.*

MCCANN (*at the door*). I'll give you five minutes. (*He exits.*)

GOLDBERG. Come over here.

LULU. What's going to happen?

GOLDBERG. Come over here.

LULU. No, thank you.

GOLDBERG. What's the matter? You got the needle to Uncle Natey?

LULU. I'm going.

GOLDBERG. Have a game of pontoon first, for old time's sake.

LULU. I've had enough games.

GOLDBERG. A girl like you, at your age, at your time of health, and you don't take to games?

LULU. You're very smart.

GOLDBERG. Anyway, who says you don't take to them?

LULU. Do you think I'm like all the other girls?

GOLDBERG. Are all the other girls like that, too?

LULU. I don't know about any other girls.

GOLDBERG. Nor me. I've never touched another woman.

LULU (*distressed*). What would my father say, if he knew? And what would Eddie say?

GOLDBERG. Eddie?

LULU. He was my first love, Eddie was. And whatever happened, it was pure. With him! He didn't come into my room at night with a briefcase!

GOLDBERG. Who opened the briefcase, me or you? Lulu, schmulu, let bygones be bygones, do me a turn. Kiss and make up.

LULU. I wouldn't touch you.

GOLDBERG. And today I'm leaving.

LULU. You're leaving?

GOLDBERG. Today.

LULU (*with growing anger*). You used me for a night. A passing fancy.

GOLDBERG. Who used who?

LULU. You made use of me by cunning when my defences were down.

GOLDBERG. Who took them down?

LULU. That's what you did. You quenched your ugly thirst. You taught me things a girl shouldn't know before she's been married at least three times!

GOLDBERG. Now you're a jump ahead! What are you complaining about?

Enter MCCANN *quickly.*

LULU. You didn't appreciate me for myself. You took all those liberties only to satisfy your appetite. Oh Nat, why did you do it?

GOLDBERG. You wanted me to do it, Lulula, so I did it.

MCCANN. That's fair enough. (*Advancing.*) You had a long sleep, Miss.

LULU (*backing upstage left*). Me?

MCCANN. Your sort, you spend too much time in bed.

LULU. What do you mean?

MCCANN. Have you got anything to confess?

LULU. What?

MCCANN (*savagely*). Confess!

LULU. Confess what?

MCCANN. Down on your knees and confess!

LULU. What does he mean?

GOLDBERG. Confess. What can you lose?

LULU. What, to him?

GOLDBERG. He's only been unfrocked six months.

MCCANN. Kneel down, woman, and tell me the latest!

LULU (*retreating to the back door*). I've seen everything that's happened. I know what's going on. I've got a pretty shrewd idea.

MCCANN (*advancing*). I've seen you hanging about the Rock of Cashel, profaning the soil with your goings-on. Out of my sight!

LULU. I'm going.

She exits. MCCANN goes to the door, left, and goes out. He ushers in STANLEY, who is dressed in a dark well cut suit and white collar. He holds his broken glasses in his hand. He is clean-shaven. MCCANN follows and closes the door. GOLDBERG meets STANLEY, seats him in a chair.

GOLDBERG. How are you, Stan?

Pause.

Are you feeling any better?

Pause.

What's the matter with your glasses?

GOLDBERG *bends to look.*

They're broken. A pity.

STANLEY *stares blankly at the floor.*

MCCANN (*at the table*). He looks better, doesn't he?

GOLDBERG. Much better.

MCCANN. A new man.

GOLDBERG. You know what we'll do?

MCCANN. What?

GOLDBERG. We'll buy him another pair.

*They begin to woo him, gently and with relish. During the
following sequence* STANLEY *shows no reaction. He remains,
with no movement, where he sits.*

MCCANN. Out of our own pockets.

GOLDBERG. It goes without saying. Between you and me,
Stan, it's about time you had a new pair of glasses.

MCCANN. You can't see straight.

GOLDBERG. It's true. You've been cockeyed for years.

MCCANN. Now you're even more cockeyed.

GOLDBERG. He's right. You've gone from bad to worse.

MCCANN. Worse than worse.

GOLDBERG. You need a long convalescence.

MCCANN. A change of air.

GOLDBERG. Somewhere over the rainbow.

MCCANN. Where angels fear to tread.

GOLDBERG. Exactly.

MCCANN. You're in a rut.

GOLDBERG. You look anaemic.

MCCANN. Rheumatic.

GOLDBERG. Myopic.

MCCANN. Epileptic.

GOLDBERG. You're on the verge.

MCCANN. You're a dead duck.

GOLDBERG. But we can save you.

MCCANN. From a worse fate.

GOLDBERG. True.

MCCANN. Undeniable.

GOLDBERG. From now on, we'll be the hub of your wheel.

MCCANN. We'll renew your season ticket.

GOLDBERG. We'll take tuppence off your morning tea.

MCCANN. We'll give you a discount on all inflammable goods.

GOLDBERG. We'll watch over you.

MCCANN. Advise you.

GOLDBERG. Give you proper care and treatment.

MCCANN. Let you use the club bar.

GOLDBERG. Keep a table reserved.

MCCANN. Help you acknowledge the fast days.

GOLDBERG. Bake you cakes.

MCCANN. Help you kneel on kneeling days.

GOLDBERG. Give you a free pass.

MCCANN. Take you for constitutionals.

GOLDBERG. Give you hot tips.

MCCANN. We'll provide the skipping rope.

GOLDBERG. The vest and pants.

MCCANN. The ointment.

GOLDBERG. The hot poultice.

MCCANN. The fingerstall.

GOLDBERG. The abdomen belt.

MCCANN. The ear plugs.

GOLDBERG. The baby powder.

MCCANN. The back scratcher.

GOLDBERG. The spare tyre.

MCCANN. The stomach pump.

GOLDBERG. The oxygen tent.

MCCANN. The prayer wheel.

GOLDBERG. The plaster of Paris.

MCCANN. The crash helmet.

GOLDBERG. The crutches.

MCCANN. A day and night service.

GOLDBERG. All on the house.

MCCANN. That's it.

GOLDBERG. We'll make a man of you.

MCCANN. And a woman.

GOLDBERG. You'll be re-orientated.

MCCANN. You'll be rich.

GOLDBERG. You'll be adjusted.

MCCANN. You'll be our pride and joy.

GOLDBERG. You'll be a mensch.

MCCANN. You'll be a success.

GOLDBERG. You'll be integrated.
MCCANN. You'll give orders.
GOLDBERG. You'll make decisions.
MCCANN. You'll be a magnate.
GOLDBERG. A statesman.
MCCANN. You'll own yachts.
GOLDBERG. Animals.
MCCANN. Animals.

> GOLDBERG *looks at* MCCANN.

GOLDBERG. I said animals. (*He turns back to* STANLEY.) You'll be able to make or break, Stan. By my life. (*Silence.* STANLEY *is still.*) Well? What do you say?

> STANLEY'S *head lifts very slowly and turns in* GOLD-BERG'S *direction.*

GOLDBERG. What do you think? Eh, boy?

> STANLEY *begins to clench and unclench his eyes.*

MCCANN. What's your opinion, sir? Of this prospect, sir?
GOLDBERG. Prospect. Sure. Sure it's a prospect.

> STANLEY'S *hands clutching his glasses begin to tremble.*

What's your opinion of such a prospect? Eh, Stanley?

> STANLEY *concentrates, his mouth opens, he attempts to speak, fails and emits sounds from his throat.*

STANLEY. Uh-gug . . . uh-gug . . . eeehhh-gag . . . (*On the breath.*) Caahh . . . caahh. . . .

> They watch him. He draws a long breath which shudders down his body. He concentrates.

GOLDBERG. Well, Stanny boy, what do you say, eh?

> They watch. He concentrates. His head lowers, his chin draws into his chest, he crouches.

STANLEY. Ug-gughh . . . uh-gughhh. . . .

MCCANN. What's your opinion, sir?

STANLEY. Caaahhh . . . caaahhh. . . .

MCCANN. Mr Webber! What's your opinion?

GOLDBERG. What do you say, Stan? What do you think of the
prospect?

MCCANN. What's your opinion of the prospect?

> STANLEY'S *body shudders, relaxes, his head drops, he*
> *becomes still again, stooped.* PETEY *enters from door, down-*
> *stage, left.*

GOLDBERG. Still the same old Stan. Come with us. Come on,
boy.

MCCANN. Come along with us.

PETEY. Where are you taking him?

> *They turn. Silence.*

GOLDBERG. We're taking him to Monty.

PETEY. He can stay here.

GOLDBERG. Don't be silly.

PETEY. We can look after him here.

GOLDBERG. Why do you want to look after him?

PETEY. He's my guest.

GOLDBERG. He needs special treatment.

PETEY. We'll find someone.

GOLDBERG. No. Monty's the best there is. Bring him,
McCann.

> *They help* STANLEY *out of the chair. They all three move*
> *towards the door, left.*

PETEY. Leave him alone!

> *They stop.* GOLDBERG *studies him.*

GOLDBERG (*insidiously*). Why don't you come with us, Mr
Boles?

MCCANN. Yes, why don't you come with us?

GOLDBERG. Come with us to Monty. There's plenty of room in the car.

> PETEY *makes no move. They pass him and reach the door.* MCCANN *opens the door and picks up the suitcases.*

PETEY (*broken*). Stan, don't let them tell you what to do!

> *They exit.*

> *Silence.* PETEY *stands. The front door slams. Sound of a car starting. Sound of a car going away. Silence.* PETEY *slowly goes to the table. He sits on a chair, left. He picks up the paper and opens it. The strips fall to the floor. He looks down at them.* MEG *comes past the window and enters by the back door.* PETEY *studies the front page of the paper.*

MEG (*coming downstage*). The car's gone.

PETEY. Yes.

MEG. Have they gone?

PETEY. Yes.

MEG. Won't they be in for lunch?

PETEY. No.

MEG. Oh, what a shame. (*She puts her bag on the table.*) It's hot out. (*She hangs her coat on a hook.*) What are you doing?

PETEY. Reading.

MEG. Is it good?

PETEY. All right.

> *She sits by the table.*

MEG. Where's Stan?

> *Pause.*

> Is Stan down yet, Petey?

PETEY. No . . . he's. . . .

MEG. Is he still in bed?

PETEY. Yes, he's . . . still asleep.

MEG. Still? He'll be late for his breakfast.

PETEY. Let him . . . sleep.

Pause.

MEG. Wasn't it a lovely party last night?

PETEY. I wasn't there.

MEG. Weren't you?

PETEY. I came in afterwards.

MEG. Oh.

Pause.

It was a lovely party. I haven't laughed so much for years. We had dancing and singing. And games. You should have been there.

PETEY. It was good, eh?

Pause.

MEG. I was the belle of the ball.

PETEY. Were you?

MEG. Oh yes. They all said I was.

PETEY. I bet you were, too.

MEG. Oh, it's true. I was.

Pause.

I know I was.

Curtain

Notes

Act One

p. 39, *down left*   indicates the position on stage

p. 39, *kitchen hatch*   window-like opening in wall separating kitchen and dining-room, used for serving food

p. 39, cornflakes   a popular breakfast cereal made of maize

p. 39, *props up*   positions vertically

p. 40, bits (colloquial)   passages or pieces

p. 40, stacked   put into a pile

p. 41, *fried bread*   at one time a popular breakfast food in Britain, made by frying bread in animal fat

p. 42, Petey's mention of the two men begins building up suspense prior to the arrival of Goldberg and McCann.

p. 42, came up to   approached

p. 42, put them up   give them hospitality or accommodation

p. 42, boarding house   a cheap family hotel, usually serving meals

p. 42, on the list   a boarding house which has been approved and subsequently 'listed' by the local council for the benefit of tourists

p. 42, turn up   arrive unexpectedly

p. 43, the Palace   the name of many theatres in England from Victorian times

p. 43, On the pier   in Britain many seaside towns built piers (iron and wood constructions) which often have a theatre for light entertainment and musical shows, as well as amusement arcades.

p. 43, Through the shouting and wild laughter offstage, without resorting to words, Pinter suggests Meg's relationship as mistress to Stanley.

p. 44, *panting*   breathing heavily

p. 44, like a good boy   a typical way for a mother to address her child

p. 44, breeze   a light wind

p. 45, off   sour, no longer drinkable

p. 45, crust   the outer part of a loaf of bread

p. 45, on the front   a promenade running parallel to the sea shore

p. 46, I bloody well didn't (vulgar)   Of course I did not (bloody is an intensifier like 'damned' and 'blasted')

p. 46, I'm off   I'm going out

p. 46, Ta-ta (slang)   goodbye

p. 46, tch, tch   a sign of disapproval

p. 46, Whoo!   an exclamation of surprise

p. 47, succulent   juicy and delicious; usually applied to food, but in this context has sexual overtones

p. 48, the strap   a leather belt for inflicting corporal punishment

p. 48, *ruffles*   runs her fingers through

p. 48, Stanley's eyes and glasses are emphasized, hinting at their important role in the play

p. 48, gravy   a sauce, traditionally eaten with meat dishes

p. 48, old washing bag   the usual term is 'old bag', a sexist term of abuse

p. 48, muck   literally 'dirt'; in this context it means that the tea tastes awful

p. 49, *recoils from*   withdraws from

p. 49, to get things in   go and do the shopping

p. 50, Stanley's pausing, the way he slowly raises his head and his failure to turn round all signal his anxiety, prior to his words.

p. 50, *grinding* reducing to small pieces; usually used for hard substances like coffee

p. 51, taking the Michael the usual slang expression is 'taking the Mickey', meaning 'to make fun of'

p. 51, *fidgets* moves nervously and restlessly

p. 51, Tell me, Mrs Boles . . . This question initiates one of the major themes of the play – Stanley's identity.

p. 52, salary payment for a regular job of work

p. 52, all found food and lodgings provided free of charge

p. 52, flying visit a quick visit

p. 52, Lower Edmonton an outer suburban area of north London and not the sort of place one would expect to find an important concert hall

p. 53, dropped him a card (colloquial) sent him a postcard

p. 53, carved me up usually used for slicing meat, or in colloquial English it can mean 'physically attack'; here 'deliberately ruined all my plans'

p. 53, shuttered up shutters are wooden boardings used to cover windows and doors

p. 53, pulled a fast one (slang) tricked me

p. 53, All right, Jack an expression of defiance; the name 'Jack', as in 'Jack of all trades' (a person who does different kinds of jobs), indicates any ordinary person

p. 53, take a tip understand a hint

p. 53, rock cake a traditional British cake of solid consistency; the usage here suggests rough affection

p. 53, pay a visit (euphemism) go to the lavatory

p. 54, Lulu a girl's name, implying sexiness

p. 54, *Ooh-ooh!* an informal way of attracting attention

p. 54, *sidles* moves furtively, with one side foremost

p. 55, Ay-ay (slang) What's happening here?

p. 55, bulky cumbersome, difficult to carry or handle

p. 55, stuffy lacking air

p. 55, *compact* a container with mirror used for face powder

p. 55, You could do with (colloquial)   You need

p. 55, under her feet   in her way, meaning he is in the house all day

p. 56, a big eater   somebody with a good appetite

p. 56, The conversation between Stanley and Lulu about going away is reminiscent of Beckett's *Waiting for Godot*: Vladamir and Estragon would also like to leave, but fail to do so

p. 56, a washout   a hopeless, inconclusive person, a failure

p. 56, Goldberg (a typical Jewish surname) and McCann (a typical Irish surname) correspond, in some degree, to racial stereotyping

p. 57, Do yourself a favour (Jewish colloquial)   Learn what is good for you

p. 57, Nat   presumably short for Nathaniel

p. 57, Take my tip   Take my advice

p. 57, regular as clockwork   perfectly regular

p. 57, Brighton   a seaside town on the south coast of England

p. 57, Canvey Island   now site of an important oil refinery, but a resort in the 1950s

p. 57, Rottingdean   a south-coast seaside town

p. 57, Shabbuss – Sabbath, the Jewish day of rest (Saturday)

p. 57, paddle   walk in shallow water

p. 57, one of the old school   a person with a traditional life-style

p. 57, Basingstoke   a middle-class town, south-west of London

p. 58, an all-round man   somebody with a wide range of interests

p. 58, coppers   coins not worth very much

p. 58, M.C.C.   Marylebone Cricket Club, the governing body of English cricket; M.C.C. was also the name used by the English cricket team when playing test matches

p. 58, my name was good   my name alone recommended me as a suitable person to receive credit

p. 58, do a job   in this context it probably means 'commit a crime'

p. 58, cool as a whistle   with perfect self-control

p. 59, The orchestration and repetition of the repartee on this page recall two stand-up comedians

p. 59, true Christian   this statement is ironical since Goldberg is so obviously concerned with his Jewishness

p. 60, assignment   mission

p. 60, aggravation (colloquial)   trouble, irritation

p. 61, deck-chair attendant   the person in charge of hiring deck-chairs at the seaside

p. 61, in all weathers   in all kinds of weather

p. 61, Does he play a nice piano?   Does he play the piano well?

p. 62, to give him a tip   in this context 'a tip' means a sum of money given for service; inappropriate in the case of a concert pianist

p. 63, the life and soul of any party   the liveliest person at a party

p. 63, cheer Stanley up   make Stanley feel happy

p. 63, down in the dumps (colloquial)   depressed

p. 63, bring him out of himself   literally 'make him forget his depression', but also hinting at Goldberg's plan to destroy Stanley

p. 66, *flatly*   without expression

p. 66, *sharply*   quickly

p. 66, *sag*   are bent

p. 66, *possessed*   dominated by a demon, Stanley's style of playing seems to suggest that mysterious forces have taken him over and his self-control has disappeared

Act Two

p. 67, strips   long, thin pieces

p. 67, Evening (colloquial)   Good evening

p. 67, *Chuckles*   quiet or inward laughs

p. 67, Many happy returns of the day   a conventional birthday greeting

p. 68, I'm not in the mood for (colloquial)   I don't feel like

p. 68, everything's laid on   everything is organized or prepared

p. 68, 'The Mountains of Morne'   popular, sentimental Irish song by Percy French

p. 68, booze-up   an occasion for drinking a lot

p. 69, Maidenhead   a town situated west of London on the River Thames; the name has a sexual connotation also

p. 69, Fuller's teashop   one of a chain of old-fashioned teashops which are no longer in business

p. 69, Boots library   a chain of lending libraries formerly run by Boots, the chemists

p. 69, thriving   prosperous

p. 69, bracing   healthy

p. 70, give it up   stop

p. 70, bloke (slang)   man

p. 71, pick on (colloquial)   choose

p. 71, Round the bend (vulgar slang)   crazy, mad

p. 71, leading you up the garden path   deliberately deceiving you

p. 71, slander   verbal abuse about somebody

p. 72, what you're at (slang)   what you mean

p. 72, flabbergasted   extremely surprised

p. 72, respect the truth   ironic, because the English stereotype of the Irish implies that their vivid imaginations sometimes make them untruthful

p. 72, draught Guinness   strong stout or beer made in

Dublin; draught means served directly from the barrel

p. 72, A mother in a million   the Jewish mother and her attachment to her family are part of the stereotyped view of Jews. Goldberg's words are sure to provoke laughter

p. 73, of a Friday   on Friday

p. 73, bird (sexist slang)   girl

p. 73, a Sunday school teacher   a lay person giving religious lessons to children

p. 73, peck (slang)   a quick kiss

p. 73, I'd bowl back   I'd go home contentedly

p. 73, tip   raise

p. 73, toddlers   young children; 'to toddle' means to walk unsteadily

p. 73, stray dogs   dogs without an owner or home

p. 73, dog stadium   an arena for greyhound racing

p. 73, Carrikmacross   an Irish market-town in County Monaghan, north-west of Dublin

p. 73, gefilte fish   a popular Jewish dish made with several different kinds of chopped fish; it is a traditional meal at the Sabbath dinner

p. 74, a game on   a game planned, scheduled

p. 74, Time's getting on (colloquial)   it's getting late

p. 74, Don't mess me about! (slang)   Don't interfere with me!

p. 74, booked out   there is no accommodation free or vacant

p. 74, at its peak   at its best

p. 75, What a thing to celebrate – birth   Goldberg refers ironically to one of the major themes of the play 'birth'

p. 75, crabby (slang)   unsightly

p. 75, boghouse (vulgar slang)   lavatory

p. 75, a dirty joke   an obscene joke

p. 75, your cup of tea   to your liking, suitable for you

p. 75, without any more fuss   without making trouble

p. 76, to get on my breasts (vulgar slang) a distorted version of the more usual expression 'to get on my tits', meaning to irritate somebody intensely

p. 76, Sit down Pinter often suggests power games behind simple actions like sitting down

p. 77, kick the shite out of him! (vulgar slang) injure by kicking him hard

p. 77, getting on everybody's wick (vulgar slang) getting on everybody's nerves

p. 77, driving that old lady off her conk (vulgar slang) driving the old lady mad

p. 78, the organization the implication is of an underground network

p. 78, Black and Tan 'Black and Tans' was the nickname given to a special force of British soldiers sent to repress the revolutionary risings of the Irish Republican Army in Ireland from 1919 to 1922; they were notorious for their brutality, and here the expression implies general hostility

p. 78, on the wrong horse (slang) mistaken

p. 78, Enos or Andrews? the brand names of two kinds of sparkling fruit salts used to treat an upset stomach or a hangover

p. 79, a fake an impostor

p. 79, Lyons Corner House one of a chain of middle-priced restaurants which existed in London until recently

p. 79, Marble Arch in central London, near Oxford Street

p. 79, throttled (slang) strangled

p. 79, skedaddled (colloquial) ran away

p. 80, left her in the lurch left her in difficulty

p. 80, in the pudding club (vulgar slang) pregnant

p. 80, an external force external, mysterious and threatening forces form one of the central themes of the play

p. 80, the proof of necessity   sophistic arguments are often used in absurdist literature by writers like Ionesco

p. 81, stuff (vulgar slang)   eat too much

p. 81, a traitor to the cloth   a priest who has broken his vows; the cloth refers to the vestments worn by a clergyman

p. 81, Albigensenist heresy   the Albigensians, centred on Albi in the south of France, were a heretical group that flourished in the twelfth and thirteenth centuries

p. 81, watered the wicket in Melbourne   in 1955, during the third test match between England and Australia at Melbourne, somebody is thought to have illegally watered the area around the wicket, causing a reduction in the speed of the ball; this was done in order to help the Australian cricketers and the scandal was reported in the national newspapers

p. 81, the blessed Olvier Plunkett   the last of the Irish martyrs (seventeenth century)

p. 81, Why did the chicken cross the road?   a well-known joke, the usual answer being, 'Because it wanted to get to the other side'

p. 82, Which came first?   'Which came first, the chicken or the egg?' – this riddle is often quoted with respect to unsolvable problems

p. 82, Stick a needle in his eye   a children's rhyme told to prove one is not telling lies: 'Cross my heart. Hope to die. Stick a needle in my eye'

p. 82, an overthrow   a cricketing term for when a fielder throws the ball in to the wicket-keeper too vigorously, sometimes resulting in extra runs being taken by the opposing side; in this context it means 'a failure'

p. 82, Drogheda   a town in Ireland and the place where many Irish Catholics were massacred by Oliver Cromwell's army in 1649

p. 82, pong (slang) terrible smell; this is later reinforced with the term 'odour' – the idea of death and bodily decay exist in these accusations, after which Stanley gives vent to his anger

p. 83, Could I have my glasses? These are Stanley's last articulate words, since afterwards he moves silently around, until at the end he makes repeated gurgling noises in his throat

p. 83, Enough to scuttle a liner Enough liquid to sink a large ship

p. 83, Scotch . . . Irish Scotch and Irish whiskies

p. 83, out on its own it's exceptional

p. 83, in the business in the tailoring trade – a typically Jewish occupation

p. 84, Walk up the boulevard pretend you are walking elegantly along a fashionable French boulevard

p. 84, torch this device suggests a kind of inquisition, which goes on parallel to the birthday celebrations

p. 84, birthday boy somebody celebrating his birthday

p. 85, 'Hear–hear' a conventional way of showing agreement during a public speech or debate

p. 85, smile at the birdy used by photographers to ask the person being photographed to smile at the camera

p. 86, the bonhomie (French) friendliness, kindliness

p. 86, Gone with the wind the title of a famous novel (1935) by Margaret Mitchell

p. 86, A little Austin a make of car

p. 86, Fullers, Boots as both have been mentioned by Stanley before, the references are sinister here, because they suggest that the two have actually met before, or that Goldberg has had information about Stanley

p. 86, knocked over very surprised by

p. 86, on our tod (slang) on our own

p. 86, kip (slang) sleep

p. 86, Mazoltov (Yiddish)   a greeting expressing congratulations, or wishing good luck

p. 86, Simchahs (Yiddish)   happy occasions or celebrations

p. 87, And well over the fast   a Jewish wish for the Day of Atonement (Yom Kippur), the most solemn day in the year, when it is obligatory to fast

p. 87, Ethical Hall, Bayswater   a lecture hall in west London

p. 87, They were all there that night   another sinister reminder of the words Stanley used when speaking about the concert

p. 87, The Necessary and the Possible   a sophistic argument; Pinter shares with the Sophists the ideas that truth cannot be known and, if it could be known, could not be communicated

p. 88, mixing them   having different alcholic drinks on the same occasion

p. 88, bouncy   hearty, noisy, but also sexual connotations referring to Lulu's young and flexible body

p. 89, King's Cross   a London railway station

p. 89, Gesundheit   'Cheers!' – German (and Yiddish) toast

p. 89, for a little constitutional   a walk taken for one's health

p. 89, rollmop and pickled cucumber   popular Jewish dishes eaten by central European Jews

p. 90, piggy-back   give a ride to somebody on one's back

p. 90, pop goes the weasel   final line of a music-hall song and a well-known nursery rhyme

p. 90, Roscrea   a small mountain village in County Tipperary, central Ireland

p. 90, Tullamore   an historical town in Offaly, central Ireland; also a famous brand of Irish whiskey

p. 90, Fenian men   during the nineteenth century, the name 'Fenian' (pre-Christian Irish warriors) was given to the men fighting for Irish freedom from the English

p. 91, Give us a song   a stereotypical Irishman is one who is always singing

p. 91, The night that poor Paddy was stretched   a line from a Dublin street ballad – 'stretched' means hanged and 'paddy' is short for Patrick, a popular Irish name and Patron Saint of Ireland; also an English nickname for anybody Irish

p. 91, 'The Garden of Eden'   popular Irish ballad by Percy French, expressing a yearning for home, appropriate to the characters in the play; Ben Clay, Coote Hill and Bally-James-Duff are all beauty spots in County Cavan, Northern Ireland

p. 91, dead image   an exact resemblance

p. 91, Hide and seek   a children's game in which one person has to find the others, who are in hiding

p. 91, Blind man's buff   a children's party game in which one player is blindfolded and has to catch one of the other players, who all stand still

p. 93, Sssh!   a sound telling somebody to keep quiet

p. 94, rat-a-tat   knocking

p. 95, *spread-eagled*   with arms and legs wide outstretched

Act Three

p. 97, run out of cornflakes   there are no cornflakes left

p. 97, splitting   terrible

p. 97, slept like a log   slept very well, soundly

p. 98, fast asleep   in a deep sleep

p. 99, rotten   terrible

p. 99, a peep   a quick or furtive look

p. 99, What are you on about? (slang)   What do you mean?

p. 100, A reception committee   a group of people formally

brought together to welcome a visitor

p. 100, Different build   physically different

p. 100, up and about in next to no time   out of bed and feeling fine in a short time

p. 101, a few letters after his name   letters indicating professional qualifications, like B A (Bachelor of Arts)

p. 101, Pure and simple   without complications

p. 102, Abdullah   a brand of Egyptian cigarettes

p. 102, a shilling in the slot   refers to the British system of a meter for operating the electric or gas supply – by putting a coin in the slot in the meter, it is possible to buy a certain amount of electricity; the meter automatically turns off when the amount of electricity has been used (today the shilling, worth about 5 pence, is obsolete)

p. 104, bust (slang)   broken

p. 104, Sellotape   a brand name of self-adhesive tape

p. 104, Monty   ambiguous, since it could be a man's name or a place; it used to be the common name for Monte Carlo, a luxurious seaside resort on the Mediterranean, known for its gambling casinos

p. 106, get it over (slang)   finish it

p. 106, knocked out (slang)   exhausted

p. 107, fit as a fiddle   in very good health

p. 107, play up, play up, and play the game   From Henry J. Newbolt's *Vitae Lampada*, once a recitation piece teaching the public-school spirit

p. 107, Honour thy father and thy mother   the fifth of the ten commandments given by God in the Old Testament (Exodus 20, 12)

p. 107, All along the line   consistently

p. 107, I kept my eye on the ball   another sporting term, meaning paid careful attention to

p. 107, follow my line? Follow my mental?   Do you follow what I am thinking? Do you follow the course of my argument?

p. 107, And don't go too near the water   And be cautious, prudent

p. 108, Benny   Goldberg gives himself a third name, adding to the mystery surrounding his real identity

p. 108, schnorrers (Yiddish, colloquial)   impudent beggars

p. 108, Seamus   the Irish form of James

p. 108, Work hard and play hard   advice generally given by teachers to students

p. 109, One for the road   referring to a last drink before a company of people split up

p. 109, You got the needle to? (slang)   Are you angry with?

p. 109, pontoon   a popular card game, played for money

p. 109, Do you think I'm like all the other girls?   a common line in seduction scenes in popular films and fiction

p. 110, Lulu, schumulu   typical Yiddish wordplay – 'schm' prefixed to a word which is repeated expresses mockery or endearment: for example, 'girls, schmirls'

p. 110, do me a turn   do me a favour

p. 110, You used me for a night. A passing fancy   a common line spoken after seduction scenes in popular films and fiction

p. 110, a jump ahead! (slang)   in a privileged position regarding experience or knowledge

p. 110, to confess   confession and the absolution of sins is a regular part of the service in the Roman Catholic church

p. 111, tell me the latest   tell me the latest news or events; strange in the context of a confession

p. 111, the Rock of Cashel   the holy site of the city of Cashel, County Tipperary, where there are the ruins of a cathedral, a chapel and a cross; royalty used to be crowned there and the rock itself is said to have been blessed by Saint Patrick

p. 112 Out of our own pockets   we will pay the money personally

p. 112, cockeyed   cross-eyed, squinting

p. 112, [You need] A change of air   advice given by doctors, suggesting that patients would benefit from a visit to the seaside, the country, etc., to improve health

p. 112, Somewhere over the rainbow   line from the popular song from the musical 'The Wizard of Oz'; there is also a proverb, 'At the end of a rainbow, you'll find a crock of gold'

p. 112, Where angels fear to tread   from the well-known saying, 'Fools rush in where angels fear to tread' (Alexander Pope, *Essay on Criticism*) and the title of E. M. Forster's first novel

p. 112, You're in a rut (slang)   you are a prisoner of a regular routine

p. 112, a dead duck   a dead man

p. 112, the hub of your wheel   literally, 'the central part of a wheel'; figuratively, 'the centre of your life'

p. 112, We'll renew your season ticket   We'll buy you another season ticket; a season ticket, purchased in advance for a set period, gives holders access to travel, football clubs, etc. at a cheaper rate than if they purchased tickets at a daily rate

p. 112, take tuppence off   give you a discount of two pence

p. 112, proper care and treatment   assurance of good service given by nursing homes, hotels, etc.

p. 113, fast days   days of fasting, when one does not eat anything, or does not eat meat; this is a regular part of some religions, including the Catholic one

p. 113, kneeling days   the days on which one kneels down to pray

p. 113, hot tips   important advice or information; often used for gambling when 'inside' information is given about the possible winner or winners of a match or race

p. 113, The prayer wheel   Buddhist revolving box, containing prayers

p. 113, plaster of Paris gypsum used for making moulds, as well as casts for broken limbs

p. 113, A day and night service typical advertising slogan, meaning service for twenty-four hours

p. 113, on the house give free of charge

p. 113, We'll make a man of you a slogan used generally as an inducement to perform 'manly' activities

p. 113, our pride and joy parents use this expression about children of whom they are proud

p. 113, mensch in German this means a human being; in Yiddish it implies a strong person who is to be admired

p. 116, don't let them tell you what to do don't allow them to dominate you

p. 117, the belle of the ball the most beautiful woman at a dance

Bibliography

Pinter's plays, poetry and prose are published by Faber and Faber, London.

Collected Theatre

(single volumes of the plays are also published by Faber and Faber)

Plays: One (1976)
The Birthday Party, The Room, The Dumb Waiter, A Slight Ache, The Hothouse, A Night Out, The Black and White, The Examination

Plays: Two (1977)
The Caretaker, The Dwarfs, The Collection, The Lover, Night School; *Revue Sketches*: *Trouble in the Works, The Black and White, Request Stop, Last to Go, Special Offer*

Plays: Three (1978)
The Homecoming, Tea Party, The Basement, Landscape, Silence; *Revue Sketches*: *Night, That's Your Trouble, That's All, Applicant, Interview, Dialogue for Three*, with the memoir 'Mac' and the short story *Tea Party*

Plays: Four (1981)
Old Times, No Man's Land, Betrayal, Monologue, Family Voices, reissued 1991 with *A Kind of Alaska, Victoria Station, One for the Road, Mountain Language*

Screenplays

The Proust Screenplay – A la recherche du temps perdu (1978)

The French Lieutenant's Woman and Other Screenplays (*The Last Tycoon, Langrische, Go Down*) (1982)

The Heat of the Day (1989)

The Comfort of Strangers and Other Screenplays (*Reunion, Victory, Turtle Diary*) (1990)

The Servant and Other Screenplays (*The Pumpkin Eater, The Quiller Memorandum, Accident, The Go-Between*) (1991)

The Trial (1993)

Poetry and Prose

Collected Poems and Prose (1986)

The Dwarfs (a novel) (1990)

Selected Interviews, Letters and Speeches

Bakewell, Joan, 'In an Empty Bandstand – Harold Pinter in Interview with Joan Bakewell', *Listener*, Vol. 1, XXXII, November 1969, pp. 630–1.

Bensky, Lawrence M., 'Harold Pinter: An Interview', *Paris Review*, n. 39, Autumn 1966, pp. 13–37.

Ford, Anne, 'Radical Departures', *Listener*, 27 December 1988, pp. 4–6.

Gross, Miriam, 'Pinter on Pinter', *Observer*, 5 October 1980, pp. 25, 27.

Gussow, Mel, 'A Conversation (Pause) with Harold Pinter', *New York Times Magazine*, 5 December 1971, pp. 42–3.

Kroll, Jack, 'The Puzzle of Pinter', *Newsweek*, 29 November 1976, pp. 75–8, 81.

Pinter, Harold, 'A Letter from Harold Pinter to Peter Wood', *Drama: Quarterly Theatre Review*, Winter 1981, pp. 5–6.

– 'Between the Lines', speech given at the seventh National Student Drama Festival, Bristol, *Sunday Times*, 4 March 1962.

Shifres, Alain, 'Harold Pinter: Caretaker of Britain's New Theatre', *Réalités*, n. 193, December 1966.

Tynan, Kenneth, 'An Interview with Harold Pinter', BBC, 28 October 1960.

Some Critical Studies on Harold Pinter's Works

Almansi, Guido and S. Henderson, *Harold Pinter*, Methuen, London (1983).

Bonino, Guido Davide, *Il teatro di Harold Pinter*, Martano Editore, Turin (1977).

Dukore, Bernard F., *Where Laughter Stops*, University of Missouri Press, Columbia and London (1976).

Esslin, Martin, *Pinter the Playwright* (first edn 1970), Methuen, London (1982).

Gale, Steven H., *Butter's Going Up: A Critical Analysis of Harold Pinter's Works*, Duke University Press, Durham N.C. (1977).

Gale, Steven H. (ed.), *Harold Pinter Critical Approaches*, Associated London University Presses (1986)

Gordon, Lois (ed.), *A Pinter Casebook*, Garland Publishing, New York (1990).

Lahr, John and Anthea (eds.), *A Casebook on Harold Pinter's* 'The Homecoming' (containing 'An Interview with Paul Rogers'), Grove Press, New York (1970)

Marzola, Alessandra, *Sospensioni di senso in scena, Harold Pinter e Tom Stoppard*, Longo, Ravenna (1989).

Quigley, Austin, *The Pinter Problem*, Princeton University Press (1975).

Thompson, David D., *Pinter: The Player's Playwright*, Macmillan, Basingstoke and London (1985).

Useful Background Works

Dutton, Richard, *Modern Tragicomedy and the British Tradition*, The Harvester Press, Brighton, Sussex (1986).

Esslin, Martin, *The Theatre of the Absurd* (first edn, 1961), Penguin, Harmondsworth (1980)

– 'The Theatre of the Absurd Reconsidered' in *Brief Chronicles*, Temple Smith, London, (1970).

Henderson, Archibald, *George Bernard Shaw, Playboy and Prophet*, Appleton, New York (1932). Shaw's letter to Henderson is dated 8 March 1918.

Harold Pinter Bibliographies

Gale, Steven H., *Harold Pinter: An Annotated Bibliography*, G. K. Hall, Boston (1978).

Imhof, Rudiger, *Pinter: A Bibliography*, T. Q. Publications, London.

An up-to-date record of Pinter criticism can be found in *The Pinter Review*, edited by Steven H. Gale and Frances Gillen, University of Tampa.